THE NEW STOUR VALLEY PATH

BY

EDWARD R GRIFFITHS

A SIX-DAY JOURNEY TO THE SOURCE OF A FINE
ENGLISH RIVER IN EASY STAGES WITH DETAILED
GUIDE MAPS AND SKETCHES

Roll on, fair Stour!   As through the fields you stray,
The Miller drains your flow to drive his wheel.
One moment lingering on your winding way,
Short gossip have with mill, then onward steal.

John Gibson, Stour Provost

BOOK ONE
(COMPLETELY REVISED)

BY THE SAME AUTHOR

THE CRANBORNE CHASE PATH - ISBN 0 9519376 2 6

THE BLACKMORE VALE PATH - ISBN 0 9519376 3 4

DORSET IN A FORTNIGHT - ISBN 0 9519376 4 2

RAMBLES FROM DORSET TOWNS - ISBN 0 9519376 5 0

HILL WALKING IN DORSET - ISBN 0 9530338 0 5

DEAD INTERESTING DORSET - ISBN 0 9519376 6 9

Nymph of the grot these sacred springs I keep
And to the murmur of these waters deep
Ah spare my slumbers gently tread the cave
And drink in silence or in silence lave

A. Pope

Grotto Spring at Stourhead Gardens

First Published - April 1994 as ISBN 0 9519376 1 8
Reprinted - March 1995
Fully Revised Edition - 1998 as ISBN 0 9513976 7 7

ⓒ EDWARD R GRIFFITHS

ISBN   0 9519376 7 7

Published by
Green Fields Books
13 Dalewood Avenue
Bournemouth BH11 9NR

THE NEW STOUR VALLEY PATH

CONTENTS

THE NEW STOUR VALLEY PATH

ROUTE MAP

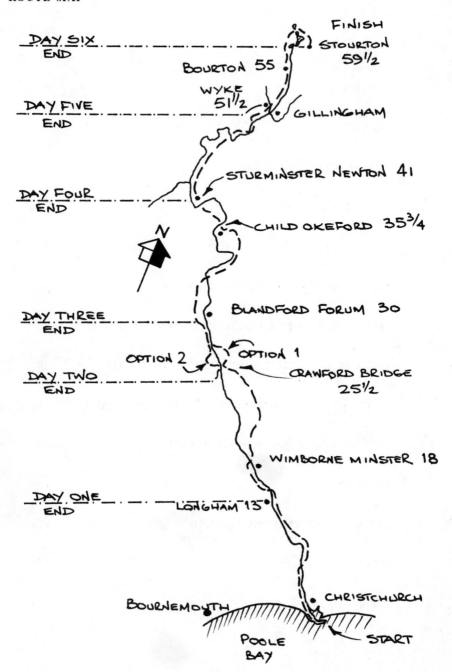

DAY SIX
END

FINISH
STOURTON
59½

BOURTON 55

WYKE
51½

DAY FIVE
END

GILLINGHAM

STURMINSTER NEWTON 41

DAY FOUR
END

CHILD OKEFORD 35¾

N

DAY THREE
END

BLANDFORD FORUM 30

OPTION 2

OPTION 1

DAY TWO
END

CRAWFORD BRIDGE
25½

WIMBORNE MINSTER 18

DAY ONE
END

LONGHAM 13

CHRISTCHURCH

BOURNEMOUTH

START

POOLE
BAY

THE NEW STOUR VALLEY PATH

INTRODUCTION

This is the 2nd edition of The Stour Valley Path and the route has been transformed in many places. In fact, looking at some of the improvements in the following list, I don't see how anybody could resist undertaking the whole journey again.

A pleasant walk alongside the River Stour from Iford Bridge to Holdenhurst replaces the boring lane round the back of Tesco's.

The primeval bog near Stapehill is avoided in favour of a direct route from Hampreston to the Fox and Hounds.

There is another riverside walk option from Eye Bridge to Cowgrove instead of having to keep to the lane.

The path to Shapwick church is now shown in detail and, on arrival at Crawford Bridge, the new route visits Keynston Mill or Spetisbury Rings (or both). The lamented fording of the Stour and the subsequent drying of feet is now avoided as the path crosses a meadow between Keynston Mill and Charlton Marshall - with bridges.

After Stourpaine, the muddy riverside path around the bottom slopes of Hod Hill can now be avoided by taking an alternative route up and over the hill fort. The original path is still included because it takes you close to the Stour but, if the mud becomes too daunting, there is even a new escape for those who decided against the new route in the first place.

After a much more detailed walk over Hambledon Hill (Hod Hill's neighbour), the road walk from Child Okeford to Newmans Drove is now omitted in favour of a fine footpath over fields, with two more bridge crossings of the Stour.

After Sturminster Newton, there is now a lovely long walk along the river bank as an alternative to the visit to Hinton St Mary. Personally, I like Hinton St Mary with its lovely stone church, its tithe barn and its manor house so the route is still in the new edition for those who can live without another riverside stroll.

After Fifehead Magdalen, the direct alternative route to West Stour has been taken out. The dash down the A30 was always a risky affair and it's much better to meander along the river's edge to Stour Provost to see the old mill and then cross the fields and the Stour again, at a beautiful pastoral spot, on your way to West Stour.

Another small change is a little diversion in Bourton so that, after a few miles without a glimpse of the young Stour, you can wander off for five minutes to view it before rejoining the others round the next corner.

'The New Stour Valley Path' is divided into six approximately 10 mile long Days instead of the original five days. Now, buses and accommodation are easier to find at the ends of Days 3 and 4 and the previously long Day 3 has become an easier ramble, giving time to indulge in a circular walk, to enjoy the sights or just to catch your breath. Now it ends with a sightseeing visit to Blandford Forum with its many buses rather than Child Okeford which has substantially less. The new Day 4 ends at Sturminster Newton, again with more buses and hostelries and, at the same time, changes the next Day from an exhausting 16.1/4 miles to a much easier 11 miles. The final Day is little changed with your triumphal entry into Stourhead.

During my wanders this time, I was accosted by a defensive sheepdog near Shapwick church and by a herd of playful heifers near Littleton.   I tried both recommended methods of dealing with the latter.   I ignored them but found they were soon treading on my heels and dribbling down my back.   Then I waved my arms at them and told them to clear off - but they enjoyed this and became even more playful - so I ran for the gate.   That worked.   I made it.   I was also eyed threateningly by three bison at Parley Court Farm and by an emu at Stour Park, Silton - honest.   I doubt that explorers of the dark continents had to contend with such dangers as these - so, when you have completed the 59.1/2 miles from Christchurch Harbour to Six Wells Bottom, you will have joined the ever-growing, brave band of "Stourists".

The River Stour has played host to many peoples over thousands of years, providing water, fish, wonderful grazing land and perfect arable conditions on its flood plains. Cereals and cattle alike have grown fat and succulent on the lush, silt-enriched land and, before it was safe enough to actually live on the edge of the river, Bronze Age, Iron Age, Roman, Saxon and Norman settlements were established on high vantage points within close walking distance of its banks.   You will pass by, through or over many such sites and more details will be given in the text as you approach them but, for now, a short list will be sufficient to whet your appetite.   Right at the start of the walk, you go over Hengistbury Head.   Then follow Dudsbury Camp, Cowgrove Roman Road near Badbury Rings, Shapwick Roman Road, Spetisbury Rings, Hod Hill and Hambledon Hill.

Many religious orders were established along the banks of the Stour, some having disappeared whilst others merged happily into the villages which sprang up alongside them to provide labour and services.   Indeed, this journey gives ample opportunity to enjoy many delightful churches of all ages and to share in the peace and tranquillity of their settings.   We pass close by many of them but several more are included where they are of particular interest and worth a short diversion.

Other communities were established alongside the fords and bridges across the river as travellers focusing on these crossings brought more and more custom to the convenient inns and stables.   Such providers of rest and sustenance were to be found in villages such as Iford, Canford, Shapwick, Tarrant Crawford (by the Abbey), Spetisbury, Charlton Marshall, Fiddleford, Sturminster Newton and Gillingham whilst innumerable flour mills were built on the Stour to provide bread for the thriving communities along the river from source to sea.   Many of the mills survive to this day and the route gives ample opportunity to visit them.

Plan your journey with the bus (and Mudeford Ferry) timetables - and the planning of a long walk is one of the most enjoyable cold evening activities, isn't it?.   The Wilts and Dorset timetables will cover the main routes but, for the rural services, you should get hold of the relevant parts of "Public Transport in Rural Dorset" published by Dorset County Council and available free from Tourist Information Centres or direct from County Hall, Dorchester, Dorset, DT1 1XT.

The Stage maps on each Day are even more detailed than in the 1st edition - but not to scale.   If you want scale, you should consult Ordnance Survey Landranger Series maps Nos. 195, 194 and 183 in that order.   You should have these maps anyway. The sketch maps only cover distances of a few yards either side of your route so, if you happen to wander off to view something that has caught your eye - or even gone wrong - you will find the O.S. maps useful to find your way back again.

Now, what are your responsibilities and rights once you venture into the countryside? Firstly, "Remember the Country Code". I know you don't need me to remind you that, if you find a gate open, leave it open but otherwise you should always close all gates behind you. We are only visitors in the countryside, especially in arable and pasture land, so take care of it. *Don't* drop litter and *do* respect the privacy of those whose cottage doorways you pass. Admiration is one thing - intrusion is another.

Beyond that, some of the rules and/or guidelines concerning Rights of Way may not be generally known and could bear outlining here:

Signposting and Waymarking: The County Council only has a duty to erect and maintain signposts where a Public Right of Way actually leaves a metalled (tarmac) road. Additionally, the Council has the power to waymark Paths and Bridleways where the route is not obvious - but it is not obliged to do so. Stiles and gates have to be maintained by the landowner where they cross Footpaths - 'to the standard of repair required to prevent unreasonable interference with the rights of the persons using the Footpath or Bridleway' - Countryside Act 1968: Section 28.

Paths through fields: Under the Rights of Way Act 1990, if a path follows the edge of a field, the surface must not be ploughed or disturbed. The law requires a minimum width of 1.5m for a Footpath and 2.5m for a Bridleway at the edge of a field. If a path crosses a field or enclosure, the path must be reinstated within 14 days of ploughing to a minimum width of 1m for a Footpath and 2m for a Bridleway.

Obstruction or loss of path: The County Council recommends that, when faced with an obstruction on the correct route e.g. lack of stiles, gates or exits from fields, make a slight deviation and report the obstruction to the Footpaths Liaison Officer of the parish in which the obstruction occurs or to the Rights of Way Section of the County Council. Such obstructions are illegal under the Highways Act 1990: Section 137.

By the way - under Section 59 of the Wildlife and Countryside Act 1981 - a bull may not be released into a field or enclosure crossed by a Right of Way unless it is less than 10 months old or, if older, accompanied by cows or heifers. Apparently, but not officially, 11 cows is the minimum safe number of cows per bull or it may still have enough spare energy to chase you.

The section on Transport Connections indicates where cars can stop either to drop you off or to stay all day near a morning bus stop so that you can walk back to the car during the Day (my own preferred system). When parking the car, make sure that you don't block any access or cause a hazard in a country lane and don't assume that pub car parks are for free general use. They are for customers so, even if you intend to have the most expensive meal available when you return in the evening, ask for permission before you leave your car in what is really a private car park. 'Transport Connections' also lists bus routes which are closely approached at various Stages so that you can break a Stage at a time to suit yourself before the end of the Day.

Now, wearing the recommended footwear (I *always* wear hiking boots for good grip and to protect the ankles on rutted tracks) and carrying enough waterproofs to be prepared for the caprices of the English weather, it's time to start at last, so go out and thoroughly enjoy yourself.

3

Oh! I nearly forgot. Before you go, I must tell you that Dorset County Council are working on their own route along the River Stour, the first stage of which was opened after the 1st edition of 'The Stour Valley Path' in the summer of 1994. This first part of the DCC route, known as 'The Stour Valley Way', reaches as far as Shapwick with onward extensions due to be opened in later stages over a period of years. Whilst the route in this book uses existing public Paths and Bridleways, the DCC's intention is to negotiate some new paths with landowners and this will delay completion of their own route until such time as all interested parties are satisfied.

You will find 'Stour Valley Way' signs and discs on your first couple of days walk as far as Shapwick, so don't be confused. Although the DCC route isn't the same as mine, I have used one of their newly negotiated sections between Iford Bridge and Holdenhurst. It's better than the old route past Tesco's. In this book, I tell you where our paths divide so that you may wander off from my chosen route if you dare - but there's always a good reason for my own particular choice, so stay with me!

TRANSPORT CONNECTIONS

Buses are mostly Wilts and Dorset but some of the local, rural services are operated by smaller companies. Relevant Timetables can be obtained from Tourist Information Centres or direct from Dorset County Council at County Hall in Dorchester. Check timetables for route times and days and take special note that, in rural areas, some of the listed buses only run on Market days.

DAY 1

MUDEFORD TO LONGHAM

STAGE	MILES	CAR STOPS	BUS ROUTES
1	0	Mudeford Quay for Ferry (Not in Winter)	121,122,123,124
2	2	Hengistbury Head Terminal	Summer Bournemouth Yellow Bus 12
3	3.25	Wick Ferry Car Park	90a at Tuckton
4/5	4/4.75	Iford Lane area	7 buses at Iford
5	4.75	Iford Bridge	- ditto -
7	6.25	Lay-by Holdenhurst Road side of footbridge	165 at Yeomans Way
9	7.75	Throop Mill Car Park	nil
12	11	Parley Cross	Choice of 5 plus 134 at Dudsbury
13	13	Longham Lay-By	X1 and 135 on Right

STAGE	MILES	CAR STOPS	BUS ROUTES

DAY 2

LONGHAM TO CRAWFORD BRIDGE

1	0	Longham Lay-By	X1 and 135
2	15.25	Hampreston village	nil
3	15.50	Fox Lane	90 at By-Pass Roundabout
4	16.75	Canford Magna	139
6	18	Merley Ways	X8, 90 and 132
8	20	Eye Bridge Car Park	320 Cowgrove
9	21.25	B/way Car Park Pamphill end	nil
10	23.50	B/way Car Park Shapwick end	nil
11	24.25	Shapwick	320 Shapwick
12	25.50	Lay-by nr Crawford Bridge (1 car)	X8, 182, 183 Spetisb'y

DAY 3

CRAWFORD BRIDGE TO BLANDFORD ST MARY

1	25.50	Lay-by nr Crawford Bridge (1 car)	X8, 182, 183 Spetisb'y
4	26or28	Spetisbury A350 with care	X8, 182, 183
5	28or29	Charlton Marshall Lay-By	X8, 182, 183
7	30	Blandford St Mary	X8, 182, 183 in Town

DAY 4

BLANDFORD ST MARY TO STURMINSTER NEWTON

1	30	Blandford St Mary	X8, 182, 183 in Town
	31	Bryanston	111 at Bryanston P.O.
4	32.25	Durweston village	X8, X94, 182, 183
5	32.75	Stourpaine	182, 183,, X8, X38, 47
6	34	Hod Hill N.T. Lay-By	X8, 182, 183 on A350
9	36	Child Okeford	303

STAGE	MILES	CAR STOPS	BUS ROUTES

DAY 4 (CONTINUED)

STAGE	MILES	CAR STOPS	BUS ROUTES
10	37	Haywards Bridge Pull-In by railway bridge	X94, 303 Shillingstone
12	38.75	Hammoon	190, 303 Fiddleford
13	40	Fiddleford Manor	- ditto -
15	41	Sturminster Newton Car Park	X94, 303, 109, 117

DAY 5

STURMINSTER NEWTON TO WYKE CROSSROADS

STAGE	MILES	CAR STOPS	BUS ROUTES
1	41	Sturminster Newton Car Park	X94, 303, 109, 117
3	42	Hinton St Mary	15, 109, 117, 190 on B3092
6	45.25	Marnhull Car Park	- ditto -
8	46.50/47.50	Fifehead/Stour Provost	46 and 48
9/10	48.25	West Stour	46, 48 and 242
12	51.50	Wyke Crossroads	20, 58, 125 in Gillingham

DAY 6

WYKE CROSSROADS TO STOURTON

STAGE	MILES	CAR STOPS	BUS ROUTES
1	51.50	Wyke Crossroads	20, 58, 125 (Gillingham)
	52.50	Milton-on-Stour	20, 58, 109 and 125
2	52.50	Milton-on-Stour	ditto
3	53.75	Silton	109
4	55	Bourton	20, 58, 109 and 125
7	56.75	Bonham	20, 58, 109, 125 (at Zeals)
9	59.50	Stourhead Car Park	20, 58, 109, 125 (at Zeals)

USEFUL NUMBERS - Correct at time of going to print.   I trust you will forgive me if they are changed:

Wilts Busline - 0345-090899   Wilts and Dorset, Salisbury - 01722-336855

Wilts and Dorset, Poole - 01202-673555

ROUTE

FOOTPATH OR BRIDLEWAY ARROW

SIGNPOST

HEDGE

WIRE FENCE

WOOD/IRON FENCE

STONE/BRICK WALL

STILE

GATE. LARGE/GATE. SMALL

BRIDGE OVER STREAM

DECIDUOUS/PINE TREE

SPECIFIC BUILDING

GROUP OF BUILDINGS (SCHEMATIC)

STREAM/RIVER

EMBANKMENT/HILLSIDE (Arrow points down)

OVERHEAD CABLES

MILES FROM START

ADJOINING MAP NUMBER

DAY 1 - INTRODUCTION

MUDEFORD SPIT TO LONGHAM

Starting at the edge of the sea at Christchurch Bay, the South Coast holiday haven, the rather long first Day's route leads to Longham on the outskirts of Christchurch's more famous neighbour, Bournemouth.   Of course, you can break the walk at any point along the way as there are ample Bournemouth Corporation Yellow Buses beetling around but I prefer to put my foot down through the built-up areas and stroll a lot slower on the riverside paths and through the villages and hamlets.   On the way, the path wanders over the Iron Age and Roman settlement of Hengistbury Head and offers a fine ramble along the riverside after Iford bridge.   Sadly, between-the-wars urban encroachment up to the river's edge drives us away a couple of times on this first Day but, mercifully, only one section has little scenic value.   Even here, compensation is offered in the form of a few welcome shops where provisions may be gathered as a treat or for sustenance for the rest of the Day.   There are two mills and another lovely riverside walk after Throop Mill.

After a last spot of urbanisation at Parley, there is another hill fort at Dudsbury (now the home of ferocious Girl Guides) and the Day ends with another lovely stroll alongside the river on the approach to Longham.

	STAGE	MILES	TOTAL MILES
1	Mudeford Spit to Hengistbury Head	1.25	1.25
2	Hengistbury Head to Wick Fields	1.25	2.50
3	Wick Fields to Tuckton Riverside	.75	3.25
4	Tuckton Riverside to Iford Road Bridge	1	4.25
5	Iford Road Bridge to Riverside Path	.75	5
6	Riverside Path to Permissive Fields	1	6
7	Permissive Fields to Holdenhurst	1	7
8	Holdenhurst to Throop	.75	7.75
9	Throop to Malmesbury Fields	.75	8.50
10	Malmesbury Fields to Parley Court Pond	1.25	9.75
11	Parley Court Pond to Church Lane	1	10.75
12	Church Lane to Dudsbury Camp	1.25	12
13	Dudsbury Camp to Longham	1	13

Mudeford Spit and Christchurch Harbour entrance

River Stour near Wick Ferry

DAY 1 - STAGE 1

MUDEFORD SPIT TO HENGISTBURY HEAD

At the extreme end of the sandbank where the tired and weary River Stour, together with its Hampshire cousin, the River Avon, flows - or rushes, depending upon the state of the tide - into the blue waters of Christchurch Bay, dip your toes into the cool sea.   Facing out of the harbour, Mudeford Quay stands on your left and, in the distance on your right is the Isle of Wight with the Needles rocks and lighthouse prominent on its West end.   Now, retreating to a safer spot, turn slowly around and enjoy the anticipation of the journey ahead before you take the first steps of your journey to find the source of this fine river.

Begin your trek on the harbour side of the dunes with soft sand underfoot at first as you pass the old, rock-protected black Watch House with its warning signs about the strong currents and the harbour speed limit.   At a little stony spit, level with some work huts, the sand gives way to pebbles and shingle and the waves lap gently against the shore as you continue.   The vague spot where the Stour enters this boating haven lies somewhere in the region of the Priory tower on your distant right.

After many private (and inhabited) beach huts, a cafe and a couple of toilet blocks, you soon pass the jetty where the ferry lands, bringing the trippers across the narrow outlet from Mudeford Quay and, even further, from the Christchurch end of the harbour.   Just past a short section of stone block defences where the sea is trying to edge in too close to the beach huts, you reach the tarmac road which runs all the way to Hengistbury Head - and here is the terminus of the Land Train - but keep walking. You've only just started and it's too early to cheat.

On past the beach huts and toilet blocks, with creeks and marsh grass now on your right, the road suddenly bends right, following the harbour edge.   This is where the first divergence from the Stour Valley Way happens.   If you want to stay at low level, this road will rejoin our cliff-top route at the car park in about 1 mile but you would not only miss the sea views and views back over the harbour but you would also stand a good chance of being run over by the Land Train.

So, at the bend, take the sandy footpath track directly ahead of you coming quite close to a few beach huts.   Very quickly, with the sea shore and more rock protections on your left, you reach a set of awkwardly spaced steps which will have you wondering whether to take one or two strides at each rise.   The route is signposted for 'Hengistbury Head Nature Reserve and Ancient Monument - No Cycling - No Kite Flying'.   Up the steps, with bracken and scrubby trees on your right, you arrive at a division of three paths with a bench facing you.

Take the left of the paths, around the edge of a fence on your left which keeps you away from the cliff edge.   There is a colourful retrospective view of the rows of beach huts and the harbour entrance from up here.   Following the seaward path, the views to Swanage and the Isle of Purbeck in the distance are extensive, from Ballard Down to Old Harry Rocks, widening as you go to reveal Corfe Castle and Bournemouth Bay.

Follow the slightly rising gravel path through the plateau of heather and bracken to an ancient iron-ore quarry dug by the Durotriges of whom more later.   After the quarry, ascend to a junction of paths and turn left at a '29' marker, heading for the distant Coastguard Lookout Station.

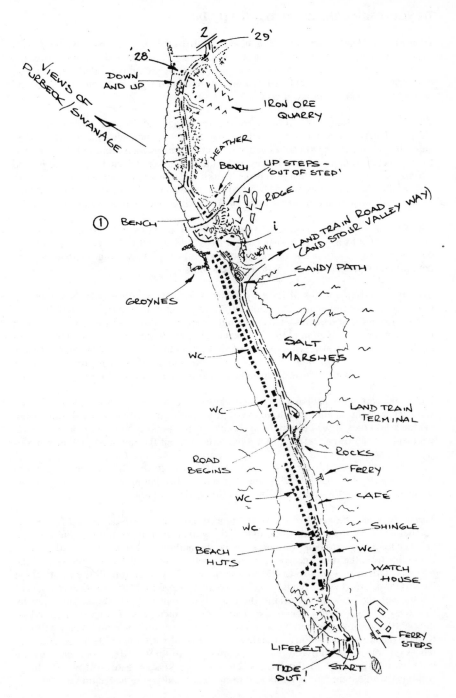

'29'

2

'28'

DOWN AND UP

VIEWS OF PURBECK / SWANAGE

IRON ORE QUARRY

HEATHER

BENCH

UP STEPS - 'OUT OF STEP'

RIDGE

① BENCH

i

LAND TRAIN ROAD (AND STOUR VALLEY WAY)

GROYNES

SANDY PATH

SALT MARSHES

WC

WC

LAND TRAIN TERMINAL

ROCKS

ROAD BEGINS

FERRY

WC

CAFÉ

WC

SHINGLE

BEACH HUTS

WC

WATCH HOUSE

FERRY STEPS

LIFEBELT

TIDE OUT!

START

11

DAY 1 - STAGE 2

HENGISTBURY HEAD TO WICK FIELDS

Hengistbury Head is the site of a heavily fortified Iron Age port where a vast export/import trade flourished.   Here, the Durotriges had settled, having journeyed from their homelands in North-West Europe.   They were highly skilled artisans who traded agricultural implements, coins which were minted right here, metallic ores and pottery for imported European goods.

They were eventually overthrown by the invading 2nd Roman onslaught under Vespasian between AD 45-47.   Before then however, such settlements were often subjected to raids by bandit tribesmen and many Durotrige men and their families left to take shelter in more secure villages under the protection of armed forces and behind massive earthworks.   Such defensive works had been necessitated by the earlier invasion by Plautius' troops in AD 43 and our route to the source of the Stour passes by and over some of these sites such as Badbury Rings, Hod Hill and Hambledon Hill.

All of these forts were eventually overcome by Vespasian's invaders and the entire West of England was under Roman control by AD 48 signalling the end of the already customary British way of life (somnolence in the face of advancing technology) and heralding our propulsion into high-tech materialism.

Your route passes a series of fences which run from the path towards the crumbling cliff tops.   Arriving at the CG Lookout Station, you will find quite a few benches scattered about near the path - and is that a helicopter landing pad just past it?   You now reach the O.S. 36.46m (119.62ft) bench mark plinth and, if you look below it on the harbour side, you will see some red rhododendron bushes - if its the right season. I wonder how they got there.   And have you noticed that there are millions of bluebells scattered all over these uplands?   A sure sign of earlier forests.

Follow the narrowing path and a few steps down the eroded sandstone end of the Head and keep straight on after a path joins you from the right.   Before a wild-life pond, the track becomes stone-coloured tarmac and, at the pond, you have a clear view on your right of the Avon and the Stour joining the harbour through reeds and marshes.

In a few yards, the path divides.   Take the left fork to the clifftop route and then, descending close to beach level, notice the reinforcing gambions and stone groynes attempting to keep the sea away from the cliffs and your path.

Turn right around the seaward end of the fenced, ancient double-dykes and follow the parallel track.   At the end of the dykes, the gravel track turns towards the Rangers Office with mown grass on your left.   Now the harbourside (and Stour Valley Way) road joins from the right and goes across your path to the Land Train Terminal and the Rangers' Office.   Cross over and follow the SV Way direction on the right of the banked tarmac road which leads to the 'Hengistbury Head Field Studies Centre'.   Turn left through the bank and, crossing the road, bear right towards the kissing gate by the 'Wick Village' sign.   Ignore the clearer track which runs off to your left and go through the kissing gate into a conservation area of scrub, gorse and small willows. Keep to the mowed path which meanders over the field with a new LH hedge and with fences on both sides until you reach a kissing gate in the far RH corner, near a wide track which turns off to the left.   Through the kissing gate, follow the long, continually undulating grass path close to the fence and young hedge on your left.

1 2

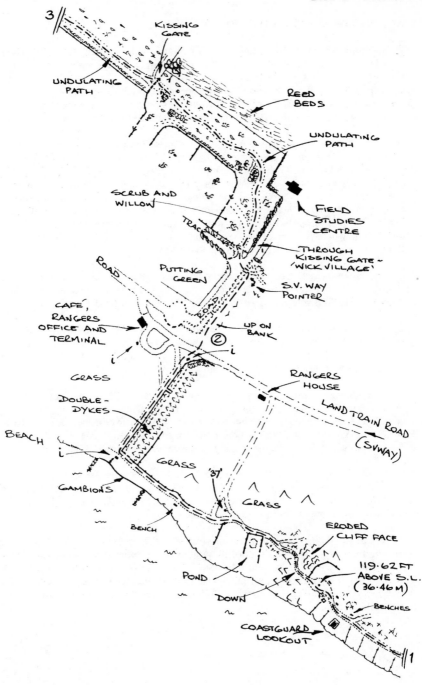

3

KISSING GATE

UNDULATING PATH

REED BEDS

UNDULATING PATH

SCRUB AND WILLOW

TRACK

FIELD STUDIES CENTRE

THROUGH KISSING GATE - 'WICK VILLAGE'

ROAD

PUTTING GREEN

ROAD

S.V. WAY POINTER

CAFÉ, RANGERS OFFICE AND TERMINAL

i

② i

UP ON BANK

GRASS

RANGERS HOUSE

DOUBLE-DYKES

LAND TRAIN ROAD

(SVWAY)

BEACH

i

GRASS

'3'

GAMBIONS

GRASS

BENCH

ERODED CLIFF FACE

POND

DOWN

119·62 FT ABOVE S.L. (36·46 M)

BENCHES

COASTGUARD LOOKOUT

1

13

DAY 1 - STAGE 3

WICK FIELDS TO TUCKTON RIVERSIDE

There are plans afoot to manage and re-landscape the area between the double dykes and Tuckton riverside (including re-siting of the Land Train/Warden's Office and the putting green) so be prepared for a possible variation of the details in this area. For now, keep following the path with the harbour edge coming closer and with masts of many anchored yachts visible just over the tall marsh grass. Go through the kissing gate in the wooden fence ahead and over the footbridge to the gate on the other side.

Now, follow the raised path between ditches to a metal kissing gate in the wire fence ahead of you. Through the gate, take the RH fork - not the one towards the houses - and follow the ridge which drops into a ditch on your right with some scrubby bushes peering over the edge of it. A S.V.Way pointer directs you down and round to another kissing gate in a hedge. Go through the gate and follow the fence-enclosed path to a final kissing gate which leads you across the driveway to the securely gated 'River House'. Keeping straight on, go through the gap in the bushes onto the riverside walk. Somewhere downriver on your right, the Avon runs into the Stour and the harbour so, from here on upstream, it's all River Stour.

The name *wick* was included in the Charters of Baldwin de Redvers about 1100 and of Richard de Redvers about 1161. It comes from the old English *wic* meaning a village or dairy farm and it is referred to as 'Weeke' or 'Week' in 17th and 18th C deeds.

Keep on the riverside path with many moorings and benches and follow the river, through a short, winding and narrow diversion past the 18thC 'Riverside Cottage' and past the old Wick Ferry gravel slip. The cottage was occupied until 1982 by a Mrs Annie Bowser with her pet monkey, Anna.

The first Wick ferry started about 1800 by a rather vague Mr Miller, at which time the nearest bridge was at Iford, a couple of miles upriver from here. In 1903, a Mr Edmunds took over the ferry, together with a hugely-built rower named John O'Brian. In 1927 this Mr Edmunds built a boat-house on the opposite bank, together with a holiday camp which later became the hugely successful Pontins Holiday Park.

Keep following the river and skirt around a fairly stagnant inlet, through trees, over a single-railed footbridge and, joining a path which comes in from your left, turn back to the river's edge. Opposite, after Pontins, is a row of bungalows and houses with their own river frontages and private moorings.

Now keep to the path past a car park on your left with a convenient W.C. and keep following the river's edge, past mooring pontoons, a putting green and a small park on your left. If you're lucky, you'll be able to get a cup of tea or an ice-cream at the kiosk. After the park, skirt anti-clockwise around the Motor Boat Booking Office from where you could catch a ferry to Mudeford Quay and the starting point for The Stour Valley Path.

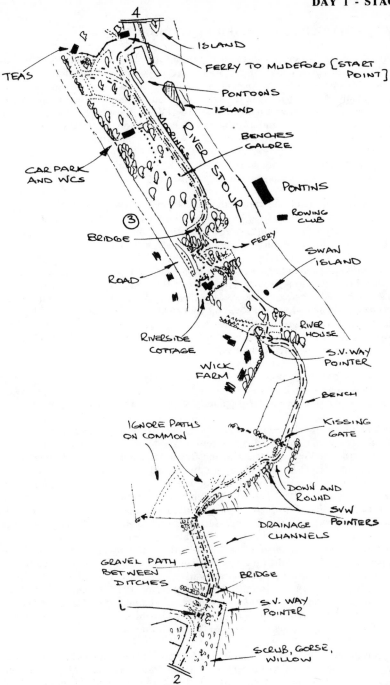

ISLAND

FERRY TO MUDEFORD [START POINT]

TEAS

PONTOONS

ISLAND

BENCHES GALORE

PONTINS

CAR PARK AND WCs

ROWING CLUB

③

BRIDGE

FERRY

SWAN ISLAND

ROAD

RIVER STOUR

MOORINGS

RIVERSIDE COTTAGE

RIVER HOUSE

S.V. WAY POINTER

WICK FARM

BENCH

IGNORE PATHS ON COMMON

KISSING GATE

DOWN AND ROUND

SVW POINTERS

DRAINAGE CHANNELS

GRAVEL PATH BETWEEN DITCHES

BRIDGE

i

S.V. WAY POINTER

SCRUB, GORSE, WILLOW

2

DAY 1 - STAGE 4

TUCKTON RIVERSIDE TO IFORD ROAD BRIDGE

After the Booking Office, go through a parking area beyond it and past several outbuildings until you reach a 'Private' footbridge on your right which links the main path with a high island between you and the main river. Past this footbridge, go up the sloping path onto the pavement in Belle Vue Road. The first road bridge across the Stour here at Tuckton was built of wood in 1881. In order to run trams from Bournemouth to Christchurch, Bournemouth Corporation built this steel bridge which opened to tram traffic on October 17th 1905. The last tram passed over it on April 8th 1936 and traffic tolls were charged here until 1943. A structural check in 1996 passed it still fit to carry heavy traffic although, during this revision, some structural and maintenance work was being carried out.

Now, cross over the road and turn left, away from the river, past the entrance to 'Riverside Inn' and past a bus lay-by. I'm afraid the next mile is mostly urban walking along pavements but just imagine the delights ahead - and you can stop and buy a few goodies in the next row of shops to enlighten the mile.

At the roundabout ahead, turn right into Tuckton Road and go past Riverside Lane to Iford Lane, just after the pedestrian crossing and the Post Office. Turn right into Iford Lane and follow the pavement, passing Donnelly Road on your left and round a left sweeping bend after Riverside Road on your right. As the pavement widens out to a short grassy verge, go through a Footpath gate in the RH fence (signed 'River Stour Walk and S.V. Way') and go down to a narrow riverside path amongst old maples and oak trees, parallel to the road.

It's only about 200 yards along here but it's relatively peaceful with traffic noises above and bird song down here for a short while. At the end of the path, go up the steps, through a kissing gate at the top and turn right onto the pavement again.

The brick buildings just down on your right are converted waterworks buildings. The plaque commemorates Count Vladimir Tchertkov and his friends. Tchertkov was the son of a wealthy landowning officer in the Royal Mounted Guard and a childhood friend of Alexander III. In 1879 Vladimir relinquished his own army career to devote his time to improving the conditions of the poor. Tolstoy's son married Tchertkov's aunt and by 1883 Tolstoy and Tchertkov were printing cheap pamphlets so the peasants could afford them. Publicising the authorities' secret attempts to exterminate pacifist peasants and to persecute religious sects, his home was raided and he was banished into exile in 1897. He chose England and came to Purleigh in Essex with an entourage of about 30 exiled professors, doctors and journalists. He moved here and established the Free Age Press in 1898. He was allowed to return to Russia in 1908 where he lived in a community with Tolstoy at Chulah, 30 miles South of Moscow. In the Bolshevik Revolution of 1917, Countess Tchertkov escaped Russia but the old Count was executed. Vladimir stayed and worked for Lenin, publishing the complete works of Tolstoy although, by his death in 1936 at the age of 82, several volumes were still to be completed.

Keep going along the pavement, past the Southbourne Tennis Club and the telephone box near the entrance to the Iford Sports Fields. Past some fine willows and one huge oak tree alongside the road, cross over to the left to walk under the brick railway arch - there isn't a pavement on your side. Then cross back again and keep going.

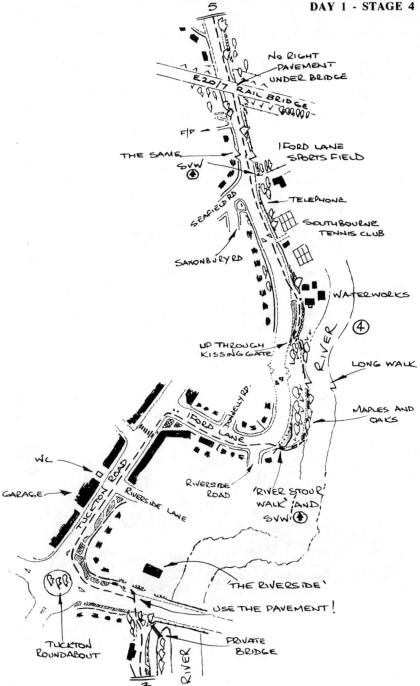

IFORD ROAD BRIDGE TO RIVERSIDE PATH

In 100 yards, opposite Collingbourne Avenue, go past the S.V.Way arrow and the gates which lead into the field on your right.   The grassy area beyond this gate provides a pleasant riverside excursion much used by the local anglers but, unless you particularly want another short diversion, keep going along the pavement and I promise you a lovely walk along the river's edge in less than 1/2 mile.

After Exton Road on your left and after the returning gates from the field on your right, keep straight on, past poplars and low aluminium barriers on your right, until you arrive at Clingan Road on the opposite side of the road.   Here, you will have reached the high wooden fence around the Iford Bridge Home Park on your right.

Just before Ashford Road over on your left, at a small bed of shrubs and flowers in the pavement, protected by black and white posts, turn right down into Old Bridge Road and follow the road past Iford Baptist Church and Old Bridge Tea Rooms.   There is a grassy area with benches by the river just before the old Iford Bridge.   Four arches span the river but many more carry the road over once-boggy grassland on the other side.   Do not go over the bridge but keep to the old road, passing another area of grass and more benches, to the present Christchurch Road with the Bridge Tavern on the LH corner.   Carefully cross the road and, towards the bridge, go between low posts on the other side to join a well-used path, with bushes on your right, across a further grassy area, signed 'Holdenhurst Village'.   A S.V.Way pointer stands higher up on your left but you're right to pick up the path here by the 'Holdenhurst' sign. You are soon joined by a path from your left and follow the River path (the one I promised you earlier) with Iford Golf Course on the opposite bank.

Old Iford Bridge over the River Stour

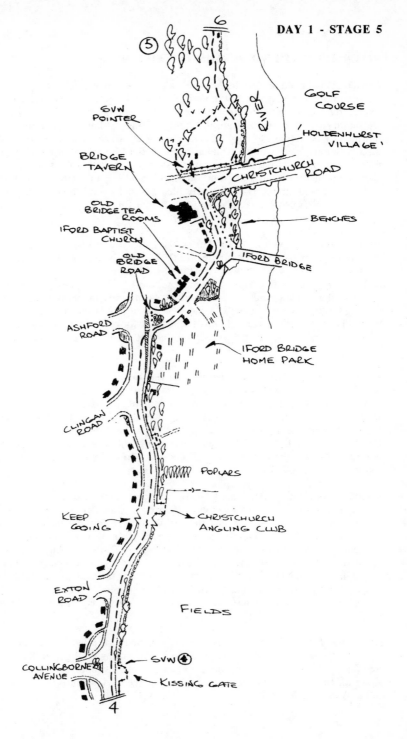

⑤

6

GOLF
COURSE

'HOLDENHURST
VILLAGE'

SVW
POINTER

RIVER

BRIDGE
TAVERN

CHRISTCHURCH ROAD

OLD
BRIDGE TEA
ROOMS

BENCHES

IFORD BAPTIST
CHURCH

OLD
BRIDGE
ROAD

IFORD BRIDGE

ASHFORD
ROAD

IFORD BRIDGE
HOME PARK

CLINGAN
ROAD

POPLARS

KEEP
GOING

CHRISTCHURCH
ANGLING CLUB

EXTON
ROAD

FIELDS

COLLINGBORNE
AVENUE

SVW ④

KISSING GATE

4

19

DAY 1 - STAGE 6

RIVERSIDE PATH TO PERMISSIVE FIELDS

Past a tree-clad pond on your left and over a concrete sluice gate bridge, keep straight on, ignoring the S.V.Way arrow pointing off to your left. A boundary sign by the river's edge shows how jealously guarded are the fishing rights along the River Stour. On the upriver side of this sign, the rights belong to Throop Fisheries whilst the downriver side belongs to the Christchurch Angling Club - and never the twain shall meet. Before Dorset County Council negotiated a route through the riverside fields for the next mile, Throop Fisheries caused Stour Valley Path walkers to lose the river shortly and also prevented us from joining its banks again until we reached Throop Mill. This next stretch is particularly pleasant and I think both Stour Valley Way and Stour Valley Path walkers should be grateful for the efforts taken to open this path to the public.

Past a solitary willow tree to the left of the path, you arrive at a stile in the fence straddling the path next to a single hawthorn bush which once gave me welcome shelter in a sudden heavy shower. After the S.V.Way arrow post, go over the stile and past the 'Permissive Path' information board. Enjoy this stroll by the river, past varying eroded banks and wild plant sanctuaries in the alluvial deposits on varying bends. By a gate with another S.V.Way arrow, where a track runs alongside the LH hedge towards a small clump of pine trees, look out for a cormorant or a heron near the rock weir. I was lucky enough to see both here - but I was *alone and quiet* at the time.

Keep following the river past reed beds in the smoother water above the weir and teasels in the river bank and across flat grassland with vast 'John Constable' skies above. Another S.V.Way arrow indicates a stile over a wire fence onto a footbridge which crosses a ditch on its other side. Go over the bridge and follow the path which turns diagonally away from the river whilst the anglers' path goes straight on. Reaching a gap in the tree-filled hedge where a grass track comes through and heads towards the river, a S.V.Way arrow directs you into the next field where you should follow the edge anti-clockwise.

Bournemouth (Hurn) Airport isn't far away and another treat awaited me just after enjoying the cormorant and the heron by the weir. Two Red Arrows were rehearsing in the skies above the Airport and their flight pattern brought them close overhead from time to time. You never know what you'll see on a decent-length walk. A whole day can hold many more delights than a short 2 miler. Anyway, follow the oak and shrub-filled RH border past three excavated areas which have me puzzled although the Water Treatment Works is only just over the next hedge and I don't like to conjecture too deeply on the significance of these 'pits'. The second 'pit' is by a big old oak which also sheltered me - on the same mixed day of sunshine and sudden downpours.

At the end of this field, go over the S.V.Way-arrowed stile by the gate and cross the short, wedge-shaped corner of the next field and, through the gap in the wire fence, turn left by the S.V.Way arrow onto a 250 yard long grass and gravel track which runs alongside the fence. The other direction carries the track towards the boundary fence of the Water Treatment Works.

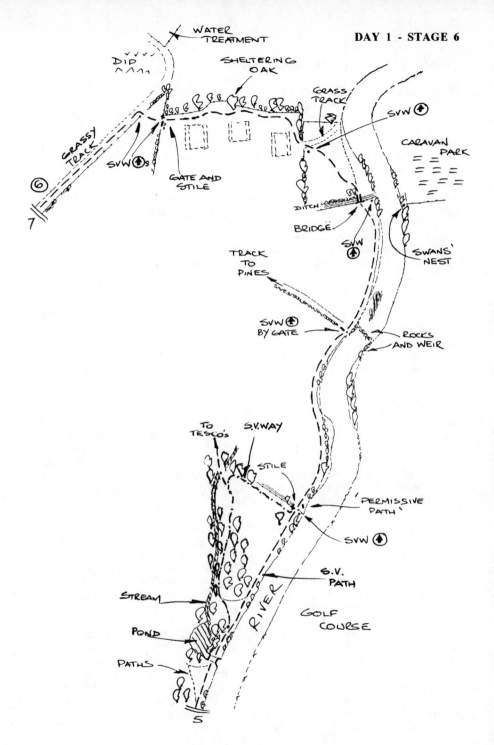

WATER TREATMENT

DIP

SHELTERING OAK

GRASS TRACK

SVW

CARAVAN PARK

GRASSY TRACK

SVWs

GATE AND STILE

6

7

DITCH

BRIDGE

SVW

SWANS' NEST

TRACK TO PINES

SVW BY GATE

ROCKS AND WEIR

TO TESCO'S

S.V. WAY

STILE

PERMISSIVE PATH

SVW

S.V. PATH

STREAM

RIVER

GOLF COURSE

POND

PATHS

5

PERMISSIVE FIELDS TO HOLDENHURST

At the end of this long track, the other track from your left is returning from the clump of fir trees.   Keep straight on past the S.V.Way arrow post to cross the small footbridge over a ditch in the wide field.   As you progress along the field edge with a wire fence and bushes on your left, another grassy track appears down on your left beyond the ditch.   Reaching a stile and a gate which lead out of your field, go past the confirming 'Permissive Path' notice into a short stretch of the lower track with a high hedge to your left.

Keeping straight on, go over the stile by the gate which closes this track, next to a concrete culvert.   The tarmac lane leads to the Water Treatment Works on your right whilst the direction from which it arrives here was the original Stour Valley Path route before the permissive path was negotiated.   Cross over the lane and go up and over the pedestrian footbridge which straddles the A338 Bournemouth Spur Road. Safely on the other side, turn right onto the tarmac lane past the S V Way pointer.

Passing the 1933 Holdenhurst Church Hall on the left, follow the lane as it bends left, past the barns of Wood Farm on the right, and you soon arrive at the Parish Church of St John the Evangelist with its fine lychgate and lantern-like bell tower.   The original village church was sited about 100 yards down the lane on the right where three cottage walls now abut the consecrated ground.   The foundation stone for the present fine church was laid on 18th July 1833 by the 2nd Earl of Malmesbury and, Bournemouth being such a 'new' town, St John the Evangelist's was the Parish Church of Bournemouth until 1845.

Originally, it had been intended that the new church would incorporate much of the reclaimed materials from the Saxon church, but it was finally decided to build it from scratch.   When it was completed, the builders credited the vast amount of £100 against the cost of the new church for the entire materials of the old one.   However, one of the bells in St John the Evangelist's is dated 1702, having been salvaged from the original, as was much of the earlier church plate and the font - so all was not lost. On the South wall inside the church hangs a unique drawing, made in 1839 by Cecilia Montgomery, showing both churches together.

Just past the church, you arrive at the fine village green which confirms the antiquity of Holdenhurst.   At the far end of the green, there are two particularly fine brick houses.   The larger LH building, labelled 'Holdenhurst Farm', is the New House which was built in the 18th Century by William Clapcott, whilst the thatched RH building is the very much older 'Old House'- quite logical really.   The Old House's deeds describe it as the former Hospice of St Mary Magdalene and it is thought to be the oldest house in Holdenhurst.

Now continue along the road with open fields on the left, mostly atop a grassy bank along the rest of the road.   An unusual feature of this stretch of road is the array of still-working gas lamps.   I hope they survive.   The first was just outside the Church Hall.   Just after another of these lamps, the RH field is bounded by a flood bank whilst a concrete ramp drops down to the gate and a prominent electricity pylon which straddles the fence into an old mixed wood.   The iron railings indicate the boundary of Hurn Court School, previously Heron Court, the centre of the vast estates of the Earls of Malmesbury since 1800.

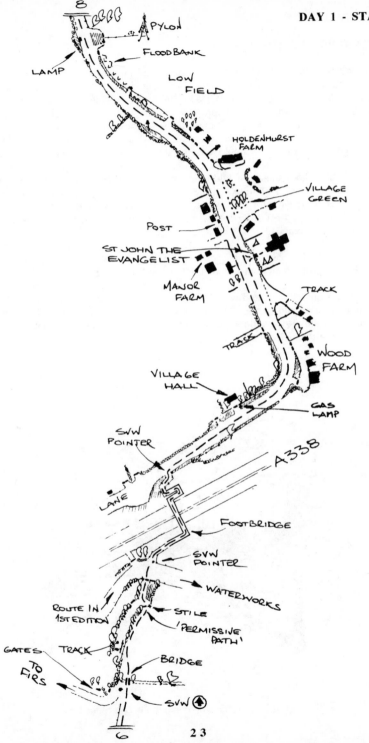

DAY 1 - STAGE 8

HOLDENHURST TO THROOP

Keep on, past the ribbon of oak, beech, sycamore and pine woods and the gated and Lodge-guarded entrance to Hurn Court School on your right. You then arrive at the Old Village School, Throop Fisheries Ticket Office and a row of cottages also on your right. The School was built by private subscription on land given by Lord Malmesbury who, with Mr Clapcott Dean of the New House, was the main subscriber. This was a good living for the teacher who earned £21 a year and who, together with his wife, lived in the adjacent School House for a rent of just one shilling (5p) a week.

Opposite the Old School stands the Old Rectory which was built in 1833 by the Rev Hopkins, the incumbent of St John's at the time, for Rev Biver, his assistant parish priest. Adjacent to the Rectory's boundary wall, the village smithy stands. Now named 'Old Forge', where Will Kefton was the smithy in 1774, the bellows and forges were removed many years ago.

After The Forge and a post box, go past the S.V.Way arrow and leave Holdenhurst Road by the signpost which confirms that you are still heading for 'Throop'.

With high fields on your left and with glimpses of our river down on your right and with scattered houses and barns (old and converted) on both sides, keep straight on past the tarmac Valley Road and the gravel Yeomans Road on your left - both heading back into the suburbs of Bournemouth.

Throop Mill from the sluice gate path - on Stage 9

24

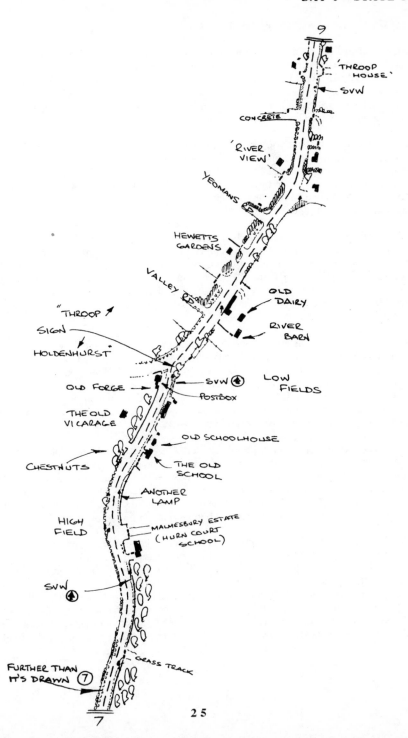

9

'THROOP HOUSE'

SVW

CONCRETE

'RIVER VIEW'

YEOMANS

HEWETTS GARDENS

VALLEY RD

OLD DAIRY

RIVER BARN

"THROOP SIGN HOLDENHURST"

OLD FORGE

SVW ⊕

POSTBOX

LOW FIELDS

THE OLD VICARAGE

OLD SCHOOLHOUSE

CHESTNUTS

THE OLD SCHOOL

ANOTHER LAMP

HIGH FIELD

MALMESBURY ESTATE (HURN COURT SCHOOL)

SVW ⊕

GRASS TRACK

FURTHER THAN IT'S DRAWN ⑦

7

25

THROOP TO MALMESBURY FIELDS

Shortly after Four Winds Farm on the left corner with Mill Road, you arrive at the huge brick bulk of Throop Mill where a Footpath signpost near the steps proclaims 'Public Footpath. West Hurn. 1.1/2'. The Stour Valley Way keeps straight on along the road to follow its own route to Dudsbury but it involves a fair stretch of main road walking later and I much prefer the meadowland, the fields, the riverside and a pair of fine farmhouses which soon follow in this other direction.

Estate iron railings lead you round and down the footpath to the back of the mill where the path turns left and follows the edge of the entrained river to the concrete path over sluice gates between the head waters and the river pool. It is only in the recent past that the route of the Stour, which used to follow this top level and was the cause of frequent annual flooding, was diverted to the route which you will soon cross by a modern footbridge.

Originally powered by water and, towards its end, by turbine engines, corn was ground at a mill on this site for nine hundred years. When the mill race was laid out to its present form in 1944, ancient stone foundations were discovered and coins from the reigns of Georges III and IV were found, together with other Spanish and Portugese coins. For a short history of the mill, have a look at the notice board in the Mill's Car Park which was unveiled by Ron Biles, the water bailiff for Throop Fisheries.

Ron Biles father, Cis Biles, was the last working miller at Throop Mill. He started work here in 1929 for Parsons and Sons whose name is still painted on the front wall. When the mill was taken over in 1957 by Heygates of Northampton, Cis continued working as a miller and stayed on when it was converted into a warehouse in 1972. The mill was truly Cis Biles' life since, at the age of 82, whilst he was painting a small window frame high up on the outside of the mill, he tragically collapsed and died, falling to the ground below, on May 20th 1981.

Anyway, passing the 'Fishing Permit Holders Only' path on your right, keep to the signed, gravel 'Public Footpath' as it turns across the open grassy area with river on either side and you'll arrive at a steel bridge across the Stour with all sorts of level controls and a weir which causes wild turbulence underneath. On the other side, turn left at the Footpath sign 'Merritown 1' and, keeping to the wire fence, cross the small bridge over a stream and a stile with a Footpath pointer on the other side.

After a pleasant stroll alongside the river, enjoying the grebes, the moorhens and the reedbeds, the path divides either side of two small wooded areas which are enclosed by low wire fences. Whichever side you choose, bear slightly right and head for the stile in the end of the field fence where it meets the river's edge. Over the stile, follow the river more closely now, with a few bushes and willows right in the water when it is running deep. If you are wondering what the roaring noise is, Hurn Airport is just beyond the fields to the North of the approaching Merritown Farm. Anyway, over the next stile by the river's edge, turn right and head across the field to the next stile in the far corner.

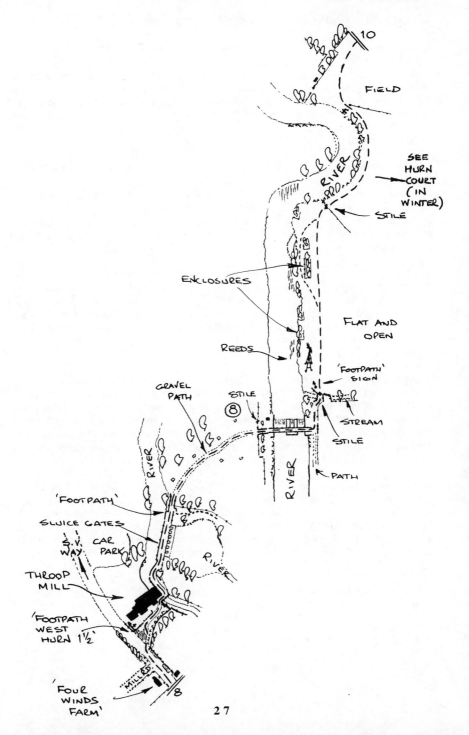

10

FIELD

RIVER PRO...

SEE HURN COURT (IN WINTER)

STILE

ENCLOSURES

FLAT AND OPEN

REEDS

'FOOTPATH' SIGN

GRAVEL PATH

STILE

⑧

STREAM

STILE

RIVER

PATH

RIVER

'FOOTPATH'

SLUICE GATES

S.V. WAY

CAR PARK

RIVER

THROOP MILL

'FOOTPATH WEST HURN 1½'

'FOUR WINDS FARM'

MILL RD.

8

27

MALMESBURY FIELDS TO PARLEY COURT POND

At the stile in the corner of the field, climb over into a very wide grassy track between high, parallel hedges.   The track is reduced to more conventional width by deep bushes and brambles.   Keep on along the track for about 200 yards with high old oaks on either side and with comfrey and nettles growing in season.   At an ancient oak wood on your left, which now sports pine trees and encroaching rhododendrons as well, the track loses its grassy covering and becomes less pleasant in the last part where the mud is frequently kept from drying out completely by the shade of the overhanging trees.

Emerging now, over a stile by a farm gate onto a junction of a left farm track and a right tarmac lane - and with a steep bank facing you - turn left at the 'Public Footpath' arrow and go past the sign on the uphill, gravel track 'Private. Merritown Farm. Public Footpath Only'.   Through the personnel gate next to the farm gate across the track, keep straight on with a descending field on your left and a complex of fun-farm enclosures on your right.   Continue straight on through the Merritown Farm buildings, taking special note of the farmhouse on your right.

The high brick house is the central section of a formerly grand house which had vast wings at either end but which were pulled down in the late 18thC.   It was part of the estates bought by Lord Malmesbury in 1800 and the farmhouse still retains some superb Georgian panelling.   Unfortunately, this is the rear of the building but the front which faces the Airport has a particularly fine Georgian frontage with a huge stone staircase and pillars either side of the main door.   The ice-house has long since fallen into disuse and has become completely overgrown.

Keep straight on through the farmyard and, as the track turns right, go over a stile by the farm gate facing you and follow an undulating route close to the banked hedge on the RH side of the field beyond the stile.   A deep drainage ditch runs parallel with the path down on your left.   When you reach another stile, by an electricity post with a yellow painted arrow, at the end of the hedge, climb over and turn instantly left to walk between the high protective bank of the Golf Course and Driving Range on your right and a hedged and fenced bank down into the field you have just left.

Follow the guard bank and the fence and keep on round to the right as you briefly come close to the edge of the Stour again.   Past the office and buildings of the Range and Golf Course, join a tarmac drive past the 4th tee.   After a fenced paddock on the RH side and past a signpost for 'Church Lane 2', the tarmac drive turns away to the right at a junction with a gravel farm track on the left.   With a postbox on the RH corner, turn right and instantly sharp left again, going through a farm gate or the adjacent half-gate across the tarmac drive which runs past a gated cattle grid.

Follow the lane alongside the RH fence and beech hedge with Parley Court Pond on your left.

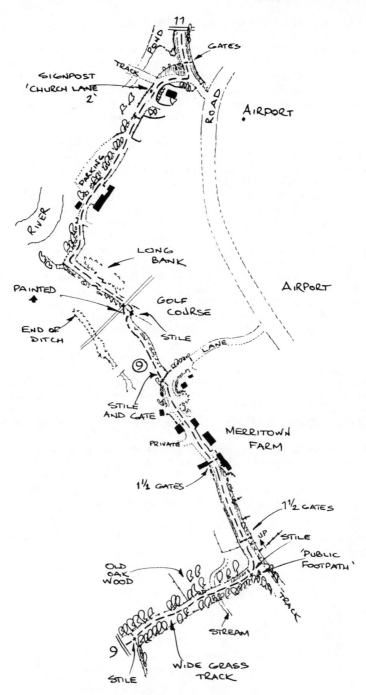

11

GATES

SIGNPOST
'CHURCH LANE
2'

TRACK

ROAD

AIRPORT

RIVER

PARKING

LONG
BANK

PAINTED

END OF
DITCH

GOLF
COURSE

STILE

AIRPORT

LANE

⑨

STILE
AND GATE

MERRITOWN
FARM

PRIVATE

1½ GATES

1½ GATES

UP

STILE

'PUBLIC
FOOTPATH'

OLD
OAK
WOOD

TRACK

STREAM

9

STILE

WIDE GRASS
TRACK

PARLEY COURT POND TO CHURCH LANE

Past the pond and a farm track which comes in from the left, go through the gate by another cattle grid and keep on the wide drive past a couple of houses on your right. This wide track, now with a ditch on either side, promises an easy walk but you have to leave it temporarily because the farm which straddles it is not keen on visitors. However, a perfectly adequate detour for walkers is provided, starting at the 'Private' and 'Public Footpath' signs by the next yard on your right.

Go into the yard with a small stable around to your right and you will see a gate at the RH end of the fence facing you with a 'walking man' sign to confirm the walkers' route.   Go through the gate into the horse trials practice area and turn left up the grassy incline around the back of a cottage.   At the top of the slope, with a leylandii hedge bordering the garden on your left, go over the stile in the fence and cross the farm track, past another 'walking man' post, into the next field which has a long brick shed as its LH boundary.

Just after a cattle trough, a stile in the fence on your left takes you back onto the wide gravel drive.   Turn right onto the track for a few yards, away from the beautiful Georgian Parley Court Farm house, and follow the track until the wire fence ends at a gate.   Immediately after the boundary hedge of the field you have just left (Field 1), there is an adjacent gate and a stile with a Footpath arrow.   Go over the stile and follow the clear grass edge of the field in front of you (Field 2).   Don't go through the inviting gap into the field on your immediate left (Field 3).

Keep closely to the hedged edge of Field 2 as it bends round left and then go over the stile by a farm gate with another yellow arrow ahead of you in the LH corner.   Along the edging fence of the next long field, you arrive at a farm gate in the far LH corner. Over the gate, keep close to the RH hedge, past three gates and a cattle trough inserted into it near its far end.   Go over a stile by another farm gate in the RH corner by another 'Public Footpath' pointer into a long farm track between high hedges.

At the end of the track, go over the stile by the gate where, by the gate on the left into Snooks Farm, a signpost confirms that you have come 1.1/2 miles on the Footpath from Christchurch Road (That's Throop Mill).   Turn right onto Church Lane, opposite Church Farm Cottages, and follow the hedged lane, past 'Stour Park' house, Brambles Farm and another fine, brick house on the left.

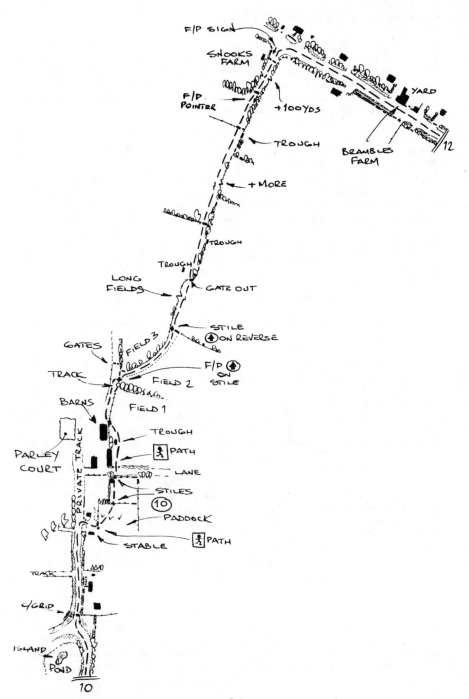

F/P SIGN

SNOOKS FARM

F/P POINTER

+100 YDS

TROUGH

YARD

BRAMBLES FARM

12

+ MORE

TROUGH

TROUGH

LONG FIELDS

GATE OUT

STILE ON REVERSE

GATES

FIELD 3

TRACK

FIELD 2

F/P ON STILE

BARNS

FIELD 1

TROUGH

PATH

PARLEY COURT

PRIVATE TRACK

LANE

STILES

10

PADDOCK

STABLE

PATH

TRACK

4/GRID

ISLAND

POND

10

31

DAY 1 - STAGE 12

CHURCH LANE TO DUDSBURY CAMP

In a few yards, the hedged turning on the left is signposted 'New Road 1/4'. Turn up this gravel track and, past the white Rest Home behind the hedge on your right, go over the stile onto a path which runs at first alongside another hedge on your left. As the LH hedge and fence run out, keep straight on across the level field with a new wire fence on your immediate right. A sign at the start of this fence implores you to 'Keep to Public Footpath'. At the far end of this field, you reach a stile in the fence. Climb over by the 'Footpath. Church Lane 1/4' pointer into New Road, Parley.

This is the last truly urban area of the Bournemouth/Christchurch conglomeration and this is where the S.V.Way comes trudging up the main road from your left and joins the Stour Valley Path, on and off, for about 1.1/2 miles before going its own way again. There is a parade of shops up the road to your right if you need sustenance for the last leg but cross over the road and turn right, even if you're not going shopping. There's a bench just along here on the verge so you can dispose of the remnants of your provisions before you finish the hike. Just past the bench, turn left into Longfield Drive and walk to the far end where a track crosses from left to right. You have a choice of two short paths from here but there's only about 200 yards involved altogether so it isn't very important. At the end of Longfield Drive, you can either:

1. Turn left and find the way through the trees into the rising field which leads up to Dudsbury Heights. In the field, dog-walkers paths go left and right. Take the right one, along the lower edge of the field and then turn up the slope to where the other path comes in from your right - or;

2. Turn right and keep straight on, past houses to right and left, to the main road. Turn left here past a bench on the near LH corner and a bus stop for the Wilts and Dorset 134. Just 100 yards up the hill, turn left into a track which instantly divides - the right fork leading to No. 243a whilst the left fork has a signpost 'Footpath. Dudsbury Heights 1/4'. After No. 244 go over a stile into the sloping field.

Here, together again, the signpost points the way to 'Longham 1.1/4', most of which is along the edge of the Stour. At the top of the hill, have a look back because this is the first high point since you left Hengistbury Head (which you can just make out in the distance on a clear day). Go through the kissing gate between the hedge and the wooden fence and cross the driveway to River Park Inn. Walk into the narrow pathway opposite, between a LH hedge and a RH fence and edging of thin trees. Now following the 6ft brick wall of the house on your left, a grassy path shoots off at right angles on your right. Keep straight on, now between a LH wooden fence and a RH chain-link fence with a lovely Victorian house and fine gardens with many rhododendrons lurking in the woods behind it. Mind the tree roots in the path here - we don't want you breaking a leg before you reach the pastoral splendours to come.

A few yards further on, go over the stile with the S.V.Way and Footpath arrows into Dudsbury Camp beyond. This is the first Iron Age hill fort on your journey but it is now occupied by the Girl Guides so I wish you luck as you gingerly cross to the other side. You are at great risk from marauding females. Now, safely arriving at the car parking area, turn right and leave by the gated and stiled field entrance down onto a tarmac driveway. Instantly, turn off the drive by going left, past several Footpath arrows on a corner fencepost, down a narrow, fenced pathway.

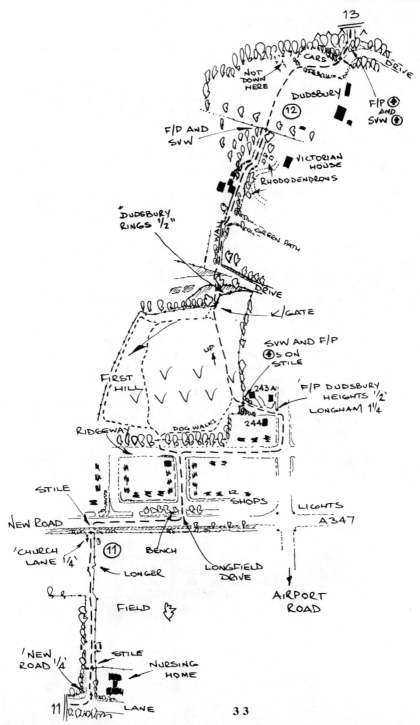

33

DUDSBURY CAMP TO LONGHAM

Although Dudsbury hill fort is scarcely recognisable now because of the encroaching houses, I'm sure you'll agree that it is still well defended - by the Girl Guides.

Go over the stile at the end of the short, fenced path between Dudsbury Golf Course and a steep, thin wood. Over the stile at the end of the fenced path, a sign reminds us that this is 'Private Land. Footpath to Longham Only' and, descending the hill between gorse bushes and the Dudsbury Golf Course, the view of the river as it meanders across the fertile plain is quite beautiful. As you drop steeply down towards the river, a glance back will show that the hill fort stands on quite a significant ridge and it would have been relatively easy to defend from this side.

At the bottom of the hill, go over the footbridge across a stream which emerges from the Golf Course and runs into the Stour. The river is divided here and both branches have pleasant weirs to break the smooth flow which otherwise typifies this stretch.

Keeping near to the boundary fence unless the river path is free of fishermen, follow the many bends of the beautiful river for 1/2 mile. On the way, the path passes between a short row of large willow trees, just after which you get a glimpse of the white-painted wooden spire of Longham Church over the Golf Course to your right. Keep going, past several reedbeds on both sides of the river, until the path almost touches the bank alongside a clump of trees sprouting from the river's edge.

Mind that you don't fall in before, sadly, the path turns away from the river in a few yards. Now, with the Car Park of the Bridge House Hotel on your left and a mowed field on your right, the path is contained between chain link fencing for about 100 yards. After bending around the brick boundary wall on your right, the path emerges into a large lay-by on a sweeping bend of the A348 from where it is only a short step to the bus stops. Plenty of buses go through Longham en route to Bournemouth and Poole or Ferndown so accommodation isn't far away. You don't have to go far, though. Longham has its fair share of Inns and Bed and Breakfasts, too.

When you come back for Day 2, just cross over to the other side of Ringwood Road (for such it is called) and follow the pavement to the left, towards Longham Bridge.

The A348 towards Longham Bridge

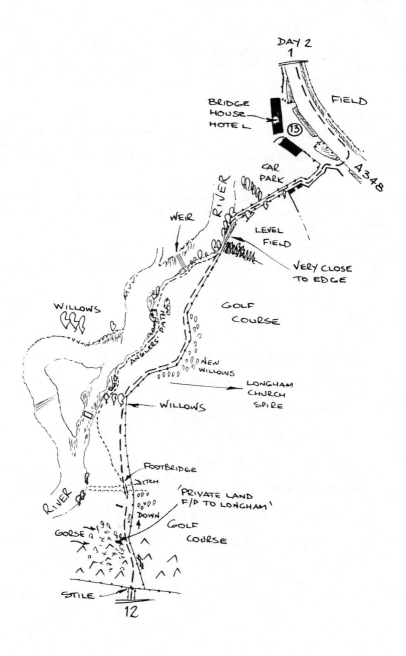

DAY 2
1

FIELD

BRIDGE
HOUSE
HOTEL

⑬

A348

CAR
PARK

RIVER

WEIR

LEVEL
FIELD

VERY CLOSE
TO EDGE

WILLOWS

GOLF
COURSE

ANGLERS PATH

NEW
WILLOWS

LONGHAM
CHURCH
SPIRE

WILLOWS

FOOTBRIDGE

DITCH

RIVER

'PRIVATE LAND
F/P TO LONGHAM'

DOWN

GORSE

GOLF
COURSE

STILE

12

35

DAY 2 - INTRODUCTION

LONGHAM TO CRAWFORD BRIDGE

A short stroll around a series of storage lakes leads to the tiny village of Hampreston from where greatly varied arable and pasture land takes you to historic Canford Manor (now a Private School) by the edge of the Stour.   A carriage drive and country lanes circumnavigate Wimborne Minster from where footpaths cross lush meadows to Eye Bridge.   This bridge crosses the River Stour next to the old Roman ford on the road between Badbury Rings and Moriconium Quay (Hamworthy, Poole).

After a lovely riverside stroll to Cowgrove Common, the route skirts the country seat of the Bankes family of Kingston Lacy, all under the protection of the National Trust. After a visit to the pretty church next to the Stour in the Saxon village of Shapwick, the path crosses meadows to the Day's end at Crawford Bridge where the River Stour flows in the lee of Spetisbury village.

This is a fine, level walk in tranquil farmland for most of the Day where birds and cattle reign supreme and where you could refresh yourself at a couple of cosy Inns on the way.

	STAGE	MILES	TOTAL MILES
1	Longham to Stour Terrace	1.25	14.25
2	Stour Terrace to Old Ham Lane	1	15.25
3	Old Ham Lane to Canford Riverside	.75	16
4	Canford Riverside to Lady Wimborne's Drive	1	17
5	Lady Wimborne's Drive to Merley Bridge	1	18
6	Merley Bridge to Willett Road	.75	18.75
7	Willett Road to Eye Bridge Fields	1	19.75
8	Eye Bridge Fields to Cowgrove Common	1	20.75
9	Cowgrove Common to Sweetbriar Drove	1.25	22
10	Sweetbriar Drove to Shapwick	2	24
11	Shapwick to Vintners Fee	.50	24.50
12	Vintners Fee to Crawford Bridge Gate	1	25.50

All Saints' Church, Hampreston

Anchor Inn, Shapwick on the Bishops Court Farm road

DAY 2 - STAGE 1

LONGHAM TO STOUR TERRACE

From the lay-by outside the Bridge House Hotel, cross over the A348 to the opposite pavement and turn left where a wire-fenced field usually houses a few ponies who would appreciate a greeting as you pass.   After a few houses and bungalows, a Footpath, signed 'Public Footpath. Hampreston Church', turns up a gravel track on your right between the last house and the Bournemouth Waterworks boundary.

The main road bridge over the Stour is worth a quick visit first, especially after heavy rain when the weir is quite impressive - but take note of the warning plaque in the RH wall of the bridge.   You don't want to be transported to Australia or - even worse - America, do you?

Through whatever gates are now current, follow the track round, past the concrete water tank on your left.   Just after the track becomes grassy underfoot, a sign warns 'No Through Road' but the track is barred now by the first indications of the gravel extraction which is the forerunner of a set of three lakes being built for water storage (and later recreation purposes).   The works are long-term and the previous cross-field Footpath has been diverted all the way around the edge of the excavations, entrained within well-arrowed wire fences.   One day, the site will be re-opened for public access and, when it is open, you should be allowed to cross straight over again (between the lakes) but, until then, follow the directions contained herein.

Go over the stile next to the gate in the hedge on your right.   It carries a Footpath arrow and a Ferndown Forest Trail arrow.   On the other side, stop and look sharp left, barely right of the line of the hedge.   You should aim just left of the last left bungalow where you will see a gap in the hawthorn hedge (NNW 336 degrees for the technical).   Arriving at a Footpath-arrowed stile in the hedge, climb over into the wire-fenced 'tunnel' with the gravel and grass embankment on your left.   You can't get lost along this path so take the chance to look around you at the fields, paddocks and the back of Longham House as you progress around the gravel pits/lakes.

Finally, you emerge over the end stile, with another Footpath arrow, into a low, gravel track.   The original Footpath used to end here, so you're back on course now.

Turn left onto the track but, in a few yards, turn right up the bank and through the RH hedge into a high field beyond.   Keep close to the LH hedge until you have passed under the overhead electric cables.   A few yards further, turn left and go over the substantial stile in the hedge, dropping down onto a sloping embankment on the other side.   Turn right and follow the undulating grassy slope alongside the high hedge for a good 1/4 mile.

The RH hedge is built on the edge of a river terrace when the Stour carved its ancient way through this level countryside and, in a few minutes, you climb up onto the terrace at a single hawthorn bush.   In January 1998, when the Stour overflowed and flooded the valley, a long line of flotsam was deposited within 6 feet of the hedge and along the bottom of this terrace, adding more substance to the old river bank.

Keep following the RH hedge, which soon becomes just a fence just before a defunct stile with a Footpath arrow and a step which serves as a seat.   A lower terrace bears off slightly to the left as you pass under more electricity cables.

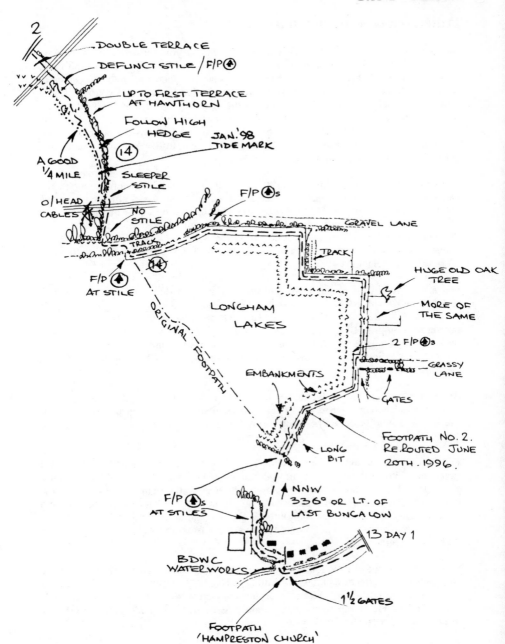

2

DOUBLE TERRACE

DEFUNCT STILE / F/P

UP TO FIRST TERRACE AT HAWTHORN

FOLLOW HIGH HEDGE

JAN.'98 TIDE MARK

(14)

A GOOD ¼ MILE

SLEEPER STILE

O/HEAD CABLES

NO STILE

F/P s

GRAVEL LANE

TRACK

(14)

TRACK

F/P AT STILE

HUGE OLD OAK TREE

MORE OF THE SAME

ORIGINAL FOOTPATH

LONGHAM LAKES

2 F/P s

GRASSY LANE

EMBANKMENTS

GATES

FOOTPATH No. 2. RE.ROUTED JUNE 20TH. 1996.

LONG BIT

F/P s AT STILES

NNW 336° OR LT. OF LAST BUNGALOW

13 DAY 1

BDWC WATERWORKS

1½ GATES

FOOTPATH 'HAMPRESTON CHURCH'

39

DAY 2 - STAGE 2

STOUR TERRACE TO OLD HAM LANE

At the end of the terrace path, with a wire fence facing you, turn right over the next stile with a Footpath arrow on it onto a narrow path at the LH edge of the high field. Follow the high LH hedge of beech trees past openings which lead into the cemetery of Hampreston Church. In about 100 yards, the hedge finishes and you will find a farm track which runs around the corner of the cemetery. Turn left and follow the track to a gate across your route. Go through or round the side of the gate into the open area beyond and follow the old brick wall which surrounds the old churchyard and cemetery. A few yards along this wall, you come to the double wooden-gated entrance to All Saints, Hampreston.

The church was largely rebuilt in 1896-97 by Romaine, Walker and Tanner in the Decorative style although a church has stood on this site for centuries. In the Domesday Book simply as *Hama* or *Hame*, the land belonged to the King but was held by three sub-holders - Aiulfus the Chamberlain; William Chernet who sub-let it from the wife of Hugh FitzGrip; and Thorkel from the King. Probably because of the connection with Aiulfus, the village was known as Ham Chamberlayne until 1293 when it became Ham Prestone.

Leave the churchyard by the same gate onto the long, wide gravel driveway which runs between a wide avenue of lime trees with a verge and ditch on the right and a wide grass verge on the left. When the drive meets the road, you will find a Footpath pointer to 'Longham Bridge 2.1/4' and a sign 'To the Church'. Bear right and cross over to the pavement which runs past the Village School and Granville Cottage on the left and continues past a postbox in the low brick wall of Hampreston Lodge on the opposite side.

At the crossroads ahead, with fields on three corners and a house on the fourth, a sign points towards straight across to 'Uddens 1/4' whilst a visitor sign points to 'Knoll Gardens'. If you've done The Stour Valley Path before, you'll be ready to cross over here - Don't.

Turn left instead along Ham Lane and cross over to the RH side where there is a pavement. When the pavement runs out, cross back again but only as far as a farm gate in the LH hedge and a gravel track to a farm over on the right. Cross back to the right where the verge is well walked (en route to the Fox and Hounds, I imagine) and keep straight on, past the lane to Stourbank Gardens on the left. Just goes to show - you aren't far from the river. You have a very pleasant stroll along its edge within the next 1/2 mile.

Still on the RH side of Ham Lane, keep going until you see Old Ham Lane over on the other side with a direction pointer to 'Little Canford'. Carefully cross back and walk down the hedged, quiet lane with a large, fenced Water Board enclosure over on your left. Follow the sweeping right bend and pass Stour Close and Stour Bank house behind the high LH hedge and trees.

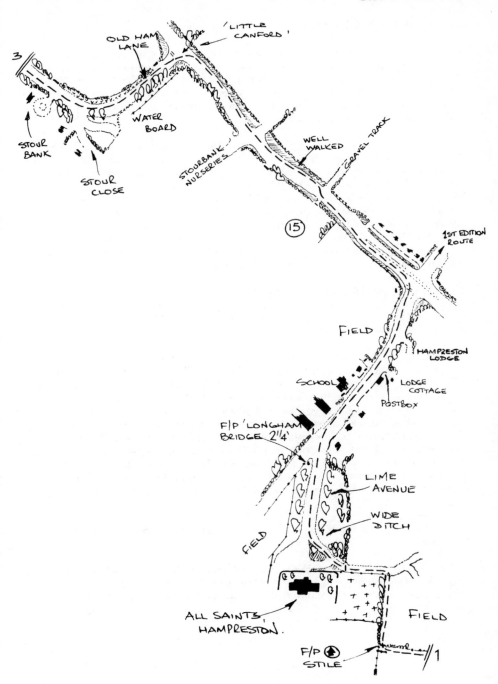

3

'LITTLE CANFORD'

OLD HAM LANE

WATER BOARD

STOUR BANK

STOUR CLOSE

STOURBANK NURSERIES

WELL WALKED

GRAVEL TRACK

15

1ST EDITION ROUTE

FIELD

HAMPRESTON LODGE

SCHOOL

LODGE COTTAGE

POSTBOX

F/P 'LONGHAM BRIDGE 2"4'

LIME AVENUE

WIDE DITCH

FIELD

FIELD

ALL SAINTS' HAMPRESTON.

F/P STILE

1

OLD HAM LANE TO CANFORD RIVERSIDE

This is Little Canford and the 'Private' high iron-fenced and gated entrance with a smart lodge on your left is an entrance to the mile-distant Canford School.   Keep straight on, past Queen Anne Cottage over on your right and past a small wood on your left.   The old exit from the Fox and Hounds is now closed by a hedge on your right but, if you are thirsty, a short diversion around the next right bend in the road will take you to this fine old hostelry.

Whether you call there or not, take note of the fine, red-brick house which stands behind the brick wall on your left almost on the bend.   To continue the walk, don't follow the lane around to the Fox and Hounds, but keep on into the straight, hedged lane with a low brick barn just on the left.   Go under the overhead electric cables and then through the double gates which straddle the far end of the lane.   Follow the banked hedge around, past the first gate to the left and, instead of continuing under the By-Pass, keep turning left and cross over the stile by a farm gate.   A pointer shows the way to 'Oakley Hill. Wimborne 2.1/4' and back the way you came to 'Stapehill 1/2' whilst a Footpath arrow and a boot with a train in it confirms that you are now on a Public Footpath and the Castleman Trail.

This 16 mile Castleman Trail path vaguely follows part of the old Dorchester to Southampton railway route which was closed in the 1960s but comes along here because much of the true railway route has been built on over the other side of the Wimborne By-pass behind you.

Now, back to the plot.   There is a wood ahead of you.   Aim for the farm gate which you will see near a couple of pine trees at the RH end of the wood, passing under the O/H cables.   On arrival at the gate, you will see a stile alongside it with Footpath and Boot arrows.   Go over the stile and maintain the same direction towards another gate and a pair of stiles which lead you onto a bridge across a drainage ditch.   Over this stile, don't head straight on towards the river - That isn't the official path.   Instead, follow the direction of the Footpath arrow and aim to the left of a solitary oak 275 yards away.   You will be walking diagonally away from the wire fence which you have just crossed over and, at last, getting nearer to the river which flows from right to left as you approach it.   By the oak, you cross a drainage gulley near to where the embankment is low enough for the cattle to have a good drink from the river and a bathe from the beach.

Just 25 yards after the beach, go over the new stile and begin a 415 yards stroll to the next one.

All along this bank, there are willows, reeds and rushes and the path is very clear and pleasant.   This is the start of a fine stretch which will be of particular interest to bird watchers and is in marked contrast to the traffic noise of Ham Lane and the near-distance By-pass.

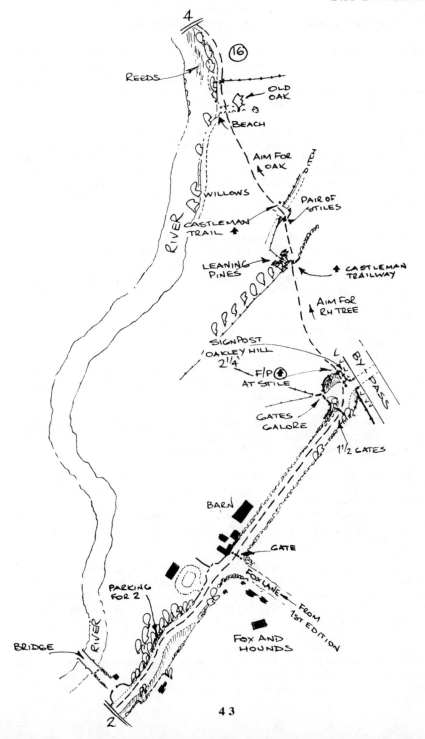

4

⑯

REEDS

OLD OAK

BEACH

AIM FOR OAK

DITCH

WILLOWS

PAIR OF STILES

RIVER

CASTLEMAN TRAIL

LEANING PINES

CASTLEMAN TRAILWAY

AIM FOR RH TREE

SIGNPOST OAKLEY HILL 2¼

F/P AT STILE

BY-PASS

GATES GALORE

1½ GATES

BARN

GATE

PARKING FOR 2

FOX LANE

FROM 1ST EDITION

BRIDGE

RIVER

FOX AND HOUNDS

2

43

DAY 2 - STAGE 4

CANFORD RIVERSIDE TO LADY WIMBORNE'S DRIVE

Cross over a stile in a gulley and a plank bridge with no handrails into the next field. Keep on along the river edge and note the terracing of the river's old route close by on your right and the two huge willows on your immediate right. Nearby is a regular nesting place for swans on the little islands. Over the river, many of Canford School's buildings now come into view - some functional, some fine and historic.

In Domesday Book as *Cheneford*, the manor was owned by Edward of Salisbury and supported two mills. The grant of Canford manor was later given to Walter of Eureux, 2nd Earl of Salisbury who died in 1196. Walter's successor, William Longespee (or Longsword) laid a foundation stone of Salisbury Cathedral in 1220 at the same time as he began to rebuild the manor house here at Canford. The oldest part of the present house is John of Gaunt's kitchen, dating back to the 14th and 15thCs, which is visible from the footpath on this side of the river.

From our vantage point, the most visible parts of greatest interest are Nineveh Court on the LH end of John of Gaunt's kitchen and the arched Victoria Tower at the other end. Nineveh Court was built in 1851 specifically to house the many artefacts brought back for Sir John Guest, the owner at the time, from Sir Austin Layard's excavation of the ancient Assyrian capital of Nineveh. Sadly, although Layard later received an Honorary Degree from Oxford University and the Freedom of London for his discovery and excavation of the "majestic capital of Assyria", it was later shown that he had, in fact, excavated the city of Calah, about 20 miles away from Nineveh. Similarly, in death, confusion over Layard's whereabouts seemed just as deep. Just before the path at the South-West corner of Canford Church stands the red granite slab of Layard's tomb on which we are informed that he was the "Discoverer of Nineveh". In fact, after a career in politics, he was cremated in Woking in 1894 and his ashes were buried there, not at Canford at all.

Now to the Victoria Tower. This was added to the house at the time of its greatest rebuild in 1848 by Sir John Barry, still for Sir John Guest, and is clearly in the style of Barry's most famous building - the Houses of Parliament.

Follow the river to another stile in a double-fence. In the next field, the path veers away from the river. Climb over the next stile in the wire fence onto a farm track and turn left and then bear right on the track by a signpost for 'Oakley Hill 1' to cross the bridge over yet another ditch. Climb over the stile by another gate into the last wide field with weirs across the river to your left. Head across this field for 250 yards to the fine suspension bridge across the river.

Across the river, take the path to the RH side of the tree - or to the left if you wish to visit the Parish Church. This is a very complicated building, never having a major rebuild or having to endure a Victorian restoration. Saxon in origin, the bulk of the church is Norman, dating back to 1120-1160, whilst the oldest identifiable section is the chancel of about 1050.

Rejoining Lady Wimborne's Drive, the former carriage drive from Wimborne to Canford, continue your journey along the shady avenue past the boat houses on your right and past a gate which leads down to the towpath used by rowing coaches on their bikes. This is not a public path, so keep to Lady Wimborne's Drive.

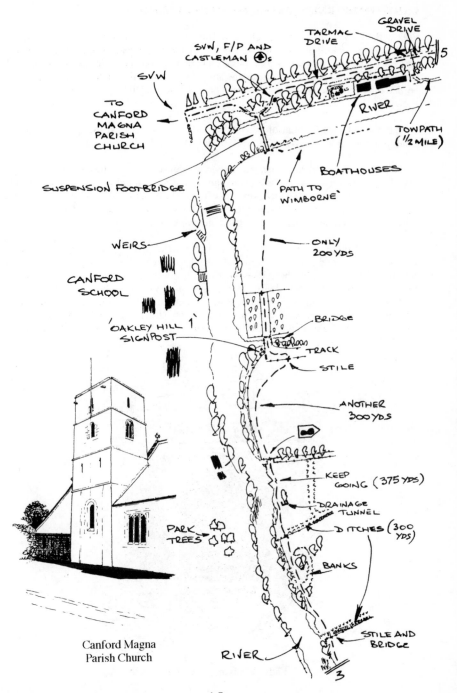

SVW, F/P AND
CASTLEMAN ⊕s

TARMAC
DRIVE

GRAVEL
DRIVE

5

SVW

TO
CANFORD
MAGNA
PARISH
CHURCH

RIVER

TOWPATH
(½ MILE)

BOATHOUSES

SUSPENSION FOOTBRIDGE

PATH TO
WIMBORNE'

ONLY
200 YDS

WEIRS

CANFORD
SCHOOL

BRIDGE

'OAKLEY HILL 1'
SIGNPOST

Badhoo

TRACK

STILE

ANOTHER
300 YDS

KEEP
GOING (375 YDS)

DRAINAGE
TUNNEL

DITCHES (300
YDS)

PARK
TREES

BANKS

STILE AND
BRIDGE

RIVER

3

Canford Magna
Parish Church

DAY 2 - STAGE 5

LADY WIMBORNE'S DRIVE TO MERLEY BRIDGE

Follow the Drive for about 1/2 mile, with lime trees closing overhead and glimpses of the A31 By-pass bridge over on your right.   After the towpath comes back through a gate on your right, you pass a rock-faced embankment on the right and walk through the concrete tunnel under the Wimborne By-pass.   After the underpass, the Drive is bordered by rhododendrons as it passes a pair of gates to left and right and a pumping station on the right.   The track is now elevated between a RH stream and a LH ditch.

By the way, I forgot to mention, the Stour Valley Way rejoined this path at Canford Church but it missed the riverside walk from Little Canford.

Suddenly, around a left-hand bend, a strange, immense structure looms incongruously ahead.   This ornate, stone-buttressed, pinnacled and shield-adorned facade would grace any Gothic edifice and it takes you completely by surprise.   This is the bridge which Lady Wimborne built to carry the unwelcome railway across her Drive.   If the railway had to intrude, then left it intrude magnificently.

Beyond this bridge, a gate and kissing gate cross the path .   A signpost points to 'Wimborne 1/2' and back to 'Stapehill 2' whilst it is adorned with Footpath and S.V.Way arrows.   Another signposted path turns off up the right bank to 'Stour Prospect View Point'.   This only affords a glimpse of the river between overgrowing bushes so keep straight on.   After a group of horse-chestnuts on the left and laurels on the right, keep straight on to a Gothic-style, stone gatehouse and leave Lady Wimborne's Drive through the double gates or one of the turnstiles.   Note the sign - 'No Cycling Please'.

Lady Wimborne's 'Gothic' Arch

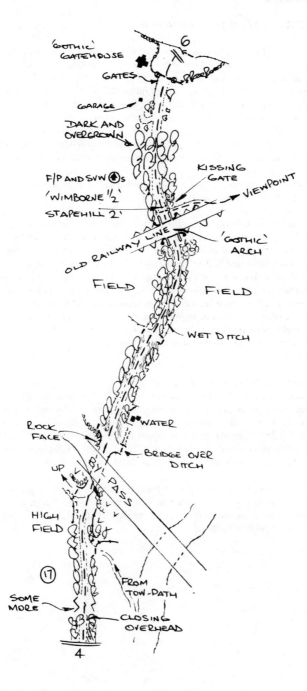

DAY 2 - STAGE 6

MERLEY BRIDGE TO WILLETT ROAD

From the wide, gravel area, go through the kissing gate onto the pavement - next to the lighting pole with 3 Stour Valley Way arrows, 2 Castleman Trailway arrows and the 'Footpath 30 and 92 Canford Magna' arrow.   Cross the busy A349 road next to Merley Bridge and, after a quick visit to admire the view upstream because that's where you're going next, come back and walk away from the river.   After just two houses, take the 'Footpath 31. Lake Gates' alley between the rows of houses, away from the main road.   Emerging onto an estate of different houses in Merley Ways, keep generally in the same direction.   Past Derwentwater Road on your left, the road bends right and then left.   Turn off into the passageway after No. 101 which is signed with a S.V. Way arrow and 'Footpath 31 Lake Gates'.   This brings you into a very pleasant, beautifully neat and grassy playground - a fine retreat for kids and parents alike on the edge of beautiful countryside.

Keep straight on up through the park and go over the heavy railway sleeper stile with S.V. Way and Footpath arrows at the top.   Follow the RH fence with the River Stour below you on the other side of a small wood.   Arriving at another S.V.Way arrow, go over this stile into a field and follow the LH wire fence along the top of a river terrace Dog-walkers follow a riverside path just below you but you all end up at the same end of this little, terraced field.   So, follow the wire fence around a LH bend to climb over another stile into a narrow path between the fenced field and a wood of hazel and oak on your right.   At the top, you meet Willett Lane where you turn right to follow the wood on your right and a banked hedge on your left   The white line acknowledges its earlier importance as a route from Lake Gates to Canford before the By-pass gave it everlasting peace.

Follow the lane around to descend along the LH bank of the By-pass to a junction of wood fences and gates at the bottom of the slope.   Through the gates, ignore the gated grass track straight ahead and go under the By-pass.   Through a gate at the top of the lane on the other side, you emerge into a turning space for cars with several Bridleway and S.V.Way arrows and a signpost for 'Footpath 31 and Bridleway 114' pointing back the way you came.   Keep straight on along the hedged lane, passing a cattle-gridded gateway, a greenhouse and some sheds on your right.

Merley Hall Farmhouse is of special interest as, between the twin gable ends of the two main parts of the house which abut the road, there resides, in much splendour, a Dutch-style gable end complete with its own resident Saint in his niche above a fine, studded, wide and superb front door.

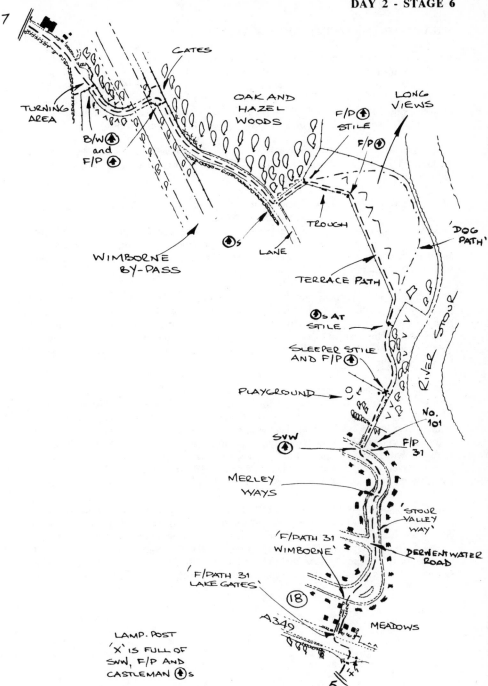

WILLETT ROAD TO EYE BRIDGE FIELDS

Merley Hall Farmhouse maintains a superb, flower-filled garden but don't spend too much time peering over the wall.   It is private after all.   Carry on past the low, brick-buttressed barn at the RH side of the road and around a sweeping bend with a deep ditch and hedge on your left and elevated cottages on your right.   The next gate on your right leads into fields behind the high hedge whilst, past a couple more house on your left, Ashington Lane turns off past a paddock - to Ashington.

A S.V.Way arrow by the Willett Road sign confirms that you keep straight on along the lane.   On a sweeping right bend in the road, the right verge widens out and a ditch appears on your left.

At the time of the 1st edition of The Stour Valley Path, the cottage on your right was derelict but it has now been restored into Lake Farm Cottage - and very pleasant too. After the Lake Farm buildings, the ditch over on your left disappears and the lane soon acquires a pavement instead.   Walk on the pavement to the end of Willett Road and then cross over to the RH corner where another pavement with a deep verge turns right along Wimborne Road as it comes down from Corfe Mullen to your left.

Another S.V.Way signpost stands on this corner.   Follow the Wimborne Road pavement down to the Wimborne By-pass roundabout and take care - it's a very busy road.   Cross over the By-Pass to the far corner and turn left to cross Julians Road. Double back a little to find the S.V.Way signpost lurking on a steep slope in the wide verge.   Drop down to the Footpath-arrowed stile and climb over - I hope it isn't very boggy this time.

A whole bundle of fences end in this corner but you are channelled through a short section on your immediate right.   Follow the top of the hawthorn-bedecked terrace until you reach a faint track coming from the gate in the roadside fence over on your right.   Bear left, down the bank, between two hawthorn bushes and aim to the right of a pair of old willows - one with a huge hanging branch (unless it's fallen off now). Here you will find a bridge and a Footpath-arrowed stile.   Go over the stile into a long, wide level field and stop.   There is a National Trust sign for the Kingston Lacy Estate on the field side of theis bridge - but more of that later.

Important Instructions - You want to turn sharp right along the wire fence to find the way across this vast open field but there is often a very wet area in your way so, what I do is walk straight ahead from the bridge for 50 yards or so and then turn at right angles.   From here, you will see a gap in the hawthorns about 200 yards away - 50 yards to the left of the only oak tree (334 degrees for the technical - or straight at the skyline pylon *without* the white cottages below it for the non-technical).   Now turn to Stage 8.

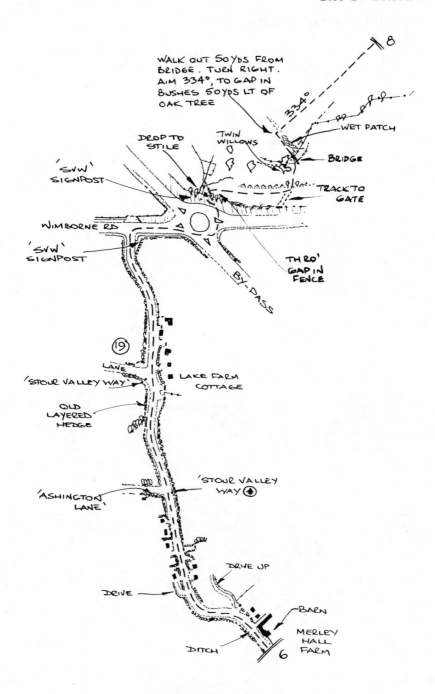

WALK OUT 50 YDS FROM
BRIDGE. TURN RIGHT.
AIM 334°, TO GAP IN
BUSHES 50 YDS LT OF
OAK TREE

334°

8

WET PATCH

TWIN
WILLOWS

BRIDGE

DROP TO
STILE

'SVW'
SIGNPOST

TRACK TO
GATE

WIMBORNE RD

'SVW'
SIGNPOST

THRO'
GAP IN
FENCE

BY-PASS

⑲

LANE

'STOUR VALLEY WAY'

LAKE FARM
COTTAGE

OLD
LAYERED
HEDGE

'STOUR VALLEY
WAY' ⬆

'ASHINGTON
LANE'

DRIVE UP

DRIVE

BARN

MERLEY
HALL
FARM

DITCH

6

51

EYE BRIDGE FIELDS TO COWGROVE COMMON

Approaching the gap, you will see a stile on the other side with 3 cottages as a distant background.   On arrival at the aforementioned gap, 50 yds from the oak tree, cross the ditch and bear slightly left towards the stile in the wire fence facing you.   A second ditch crosses your path before the stile.

Over the stile, follow a due-North path across the next vast field, aiming for a single hawthorn bush and the wire fence corner post.   Aim for the highest cottage on the hill ahead (the only one without a thatched roof).   At the corner post, you will find Footpath and SVWay arrows.   Now, choose a route which takes you progressively away from the wire fence (18 degrees from North) towards the far distant end of the long, narrowing field.   In the far corner, you will find a stile with a Footpath arrow. Go over and follow the LH wire fence to the steps up onto Eye Bridge.

From up here, there are superb views along the River Stour towards Wimborne.   The Roman ford is still clearly visible and is still in use (by tractors).   When you leave the bridge, you have a choice of two routes.   If you would like a stroll along the river to Cowgrove, turn left over the stile as soon as you leave the bridge but, if you would prefer an easier route, with no stiles, along the Cowgrove road, turn right and walk along to the parking area to the left of the ford.   Now, follow your own pertinent instructions below:

RIVER: Over the stile, follow the wide grassy path between the RH wire fence and the tree-clad bank of the meandering River Stour.   Keep an eye open for kingfishers and herons - you'll see neither unless you're absolutely silent.   After a bridge and stile, the river has deposited a growing island on this side whilst it is still undercutting on the outer sweeps of its bends.   Over the next stile, next to a gate, three paths present themselves.   Turn sharp right and follow the edge of the wire fence with the second path below you through the trees and bushes.   A few zig-zags follow the fence until you find a suitable spot to drop down to the lower path when it isn't boggy any more.   After a 'Private' gate, the path bends round to the left and arrives at a little bridge and stile which leads out onto Cowgrove Common.   Follow the RH hedge around to cross a ditch by a another small bridge and follow the path past a Footpath sign.   Cross Cowgrove road and walk around the left end of three poplars, by a lovely duckpond.   Bear left onto a gravel track past Poplar Farm.

ROAD: Leave the Eye Mead car park and turn left onto the road.   Keep straight on past the two right turnings and the low hedge allows good views over the lush river valley farmland.   After the recently restored Old Court House and Lower Dairy Cottage on your left and Walnut Farm on your right, you pass the barns of the Old Lower Dairy.   Next to the Firs Farmhouse, there is a rare grain store supported by rat-defeating staddle stones.   It's good to see them being used for their original purpose. In a few more yards, you reach Cowgrove Common where a Footpath arrow points left past the thatched Drews Cottage.   Bear off to the right here past three tall poplars and follow the gravel track which runs between the duckpond and Poplar Farm.

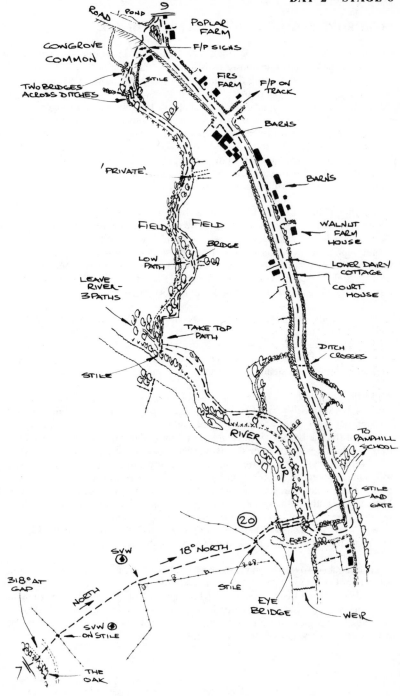

ROAD
POND
POPLAR FARM
F/P SIGNS
COWGROVE COMMON
FIRS FARM
F/P ON TRACK
STILE
TWO BRIDGES ACROSS DITCHES
BARNS
BARNS
'PRIVATE'
WALNUT FARM HOUSE
FIELD
FIELD
BRIDGE
LOWER DAIRY COTTAGE
LOW PATH
COURT HOUSE
LEAVE RIVER - 3 PATHS
DITCH CROSSES
TAKE TOP PATH
STILE
TO PAMPHILL SCHOOL
RIVER STOUR
STILE AND GATE
⑳
18° NORTH
SVW
FORD
318° AT GAP
STILE
NORTH
EYE BRIDGE
WEIR
SVW ON STILE
THE OAK

COWGROVE COMMON TO SWEETBRIAR DROVE

Go through the gate across the track with Bridleway and Footpath arrows pointing into the RH field. The track now bends round to the right with a RH hedge and a LH wood fence. Keep following the track, now becoming more grassy, past a thatched cottage and past a RH open area. Here begins Little Cowgrove Common which is shown on old tithe maps as bordered by cottages but they are no longer in existence. Now, across the common, you will see a row of four pairs of white cottages. A signed Footpath goes off over a stile on your right but ignore it and keep straight on, past a fence-protected oak, to a tiled house with a barn at the rear. Just past the house, All Fools Lane leads up to the fine cricket pitch, pavilion and beech avenue of Pamphill Village Green - all still part of the Kingston Lacy Estate. However, keep straight on, past the Bridleway sign, to join the road ahead.

Turn right and keep to the RH edge of the road which has verges on both sides at first. Passing beneath O/H electric cables and by a group of new trees on the right, keep on the road which now has beech hedges on both sides. After a few bends and going slightly uphill, the road verges disappear and so do the ditches, so be careful for 100 yards as you are confined by close beech hedges with a small pine and deciduous wood on your right. Soon, you reach a sharp RH bend with a high bank on the right topped with a birch, oak and beech hedge on the corner.

Cross over to the left and, by a Bridleway and a S.V.Way pointer, turn into the wide entrance to the track which goes all round the perimeter of Kingston Lacy Park. Go through the 'Emergency Fire Access' gate after the parking area for a few cars and, with a verge, a ditch and a hedge on your left, start on the long Bridleway, past the well-kept garden of a small estate cottage on your right.

All of the great trees on your right are bordering Kingston Lacy Park and numerous signs on the way will remind you that the estate is very 'Private' unless you come in through the front gates and pay for your admission. Now with some grass up the middle of the track, start slightly uphill and pass under the branches of a huge beech tree which hangs right over the Bridleway from beyond the ditch on your right. With ditches, bushes and wire fences alternating along the edges of the track, go round the RH bend in the track and pass the three-way Bridleway sign where a wide, grassy track takes the S.V.Way walkers off to your left on the way down to White Mill and the path to Shapwick. I prefer to stay higher up for the next 1.1/2 miles because the views are superb over the Stour valley from up here and it is much quieter as well - and you can see Badbury Rings and walk down the Roman road which ran from Salisbury, past the Rings and down to ford the Stour at Shapwick.

Keep straight on to the second three-way Bridleway sign and turn left this time - into Sweetbriar Drove. On both sides of this wide, grassy track, there are old and new ash, oak and beech trees, evenly spaced along the hedges whilst, over on your right, you can see the heights of Badbury Rings, the Iron age hill settlement. Now, after a myriad of farm gates to left, right and centre, just keep straight on along the track with fine views ahead into the Stour Valley.

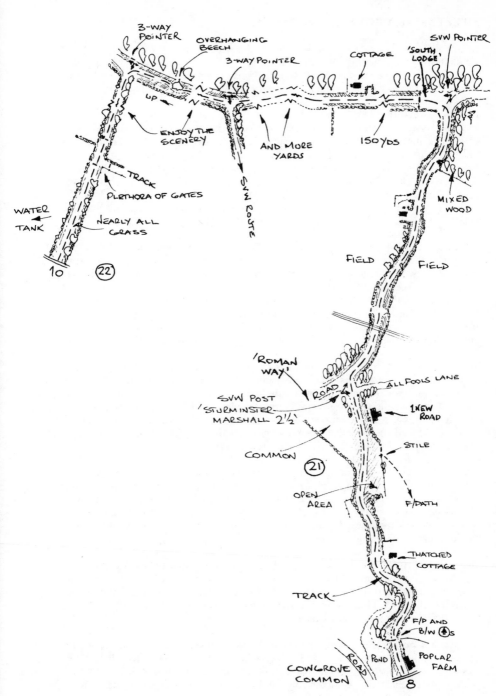

3-WAY POINTER

OVERHANGING BEECH

3-WAY POINTER

SVW POINTER

COTTAGE

'SOUTH LODGE'

UP

ENJOY THE SCENERY

AND MORE YARDS

150 YDS

MIXED WOOD

TRACK

PLETHORA OF GATES

SVW ROUTE

WATER TANK

NEARLY ALL GRASS

10   (22)

FIELD

FIELD

'ROMAN WAY'

ROAD

ALL FOOLS LANE

SVW POST 'STURMINSTER MARSHALL 2½'

1 NEW ROAD

COMMON

STILE

(21)

OPEN AREA

F/PATH

THATCHED COTTAGE

TRACK

F/P AND B/W (4)s

COWGROVE COMMON

ROAD

POND

POPLAR FARM

8

SWEETBRIAR DROVE TO SHAPWICK

Keep going, past a new wood on your left and a wide, grassy, signposted Bridleway which turns off to Badbury Rings on your right.   On your right, you will see the 1 mile long beech avenue on the B3082 Blandford Forum to Wimborne Minster road which leads the way to the original main gates for Kingston Lacy House.

Leaving Sweetbriar Drove through the gate, take care crossing the Sturminster Marshall road.   On your left is the sign for 'Shapwick' and, on the far corner of the crossroads, it says 'Park Lane'.   You can still change your mind and go down the road to White Mill and join the S.V. Way if you like.   But, if you're coming with me, take the lane opposite and keep straight on.   In about 100 yards, at the top of the rise, there are fine views into the Stour Valley and across to the folly tower at Charborough Park on the left but higher ground on the right restricts the view temporarily in this direction.   Soon, on the right, at a new small wood and two large beeches, the field becomes somewhat lower and better views towards Badbury Rings appear.

On the left, after an open-fronted equipment storage barn, the buildings of New Barn Farm abut the road, followed by the fine farmhouse behind a low, castellated stone wall and a row of staddle stones.   Arriving at a row of new sycamores on the right, the view into the valley becomes even more extensive and, for this reason, we will stay on this road for another 1/2 mile when we arrive at the gravel Bridleway on the left in a few yards.   Up here, the sound of skylarks is encouraging since modern pesticides are causing their depletion in other areas.   If you are here in May, the smell of the cow-parsley in the deep verges is superb and rather heady.

Just after the small wood on the right, a track goes down into an old chalk quarry, also on the right.   Just after this track, there is a row of large beeches on the right and, on the left, a long row of newly planted individual sycamores has been introduced into the hedgerow all the way to the next farm complex on the left.   Arriving at O/H electric wires which cross the road above high hedges to left and right, take care for the next 100 yards because there are no verges.   However, Crab Farm is just around the bend to the left and there is a very wide forecourt to run into if necessary.

At the crossroads, with Queen Cottages on the RH corner with Ram Lane, turn left into 'High Street' which appears to be somewhat inappropriately named as we now leave the high ground and take the gently sloping downhill road into Shapwick. This is the Roman road I mentioned earlier which comes down from Badbury Rings and a 1 mile trip up this road would bring you to the Rings.   However, continue down the road, past Hyde Farm on your right.

Incidentally, listed as *Sceapwic* in the Domesday Book and owned by the King, Shapwick gets its name from the Saxon *sceap* meaning sheep and *wic* meaning village (as mentioned at Wick on Day 1).   This was serious sheep country until 1922 when the Shapwick Flock, which was established back in 1834 and the last great sheep flock in the area, was disbanded.

There was a terrible fire here on October 14th 1881.   It started behind the old inn and spread rapidly through the thatched cottages in a high wind.   Sixteen homes were destroyed and eighty-five people made homeless but nobody was killed.   In 1882, some replacement houses were built by the Bankes of Kingston Lacy in High Street.

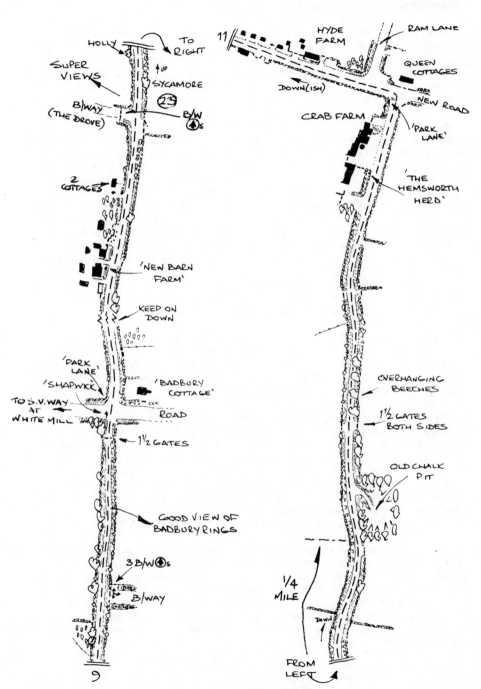

HOLLY

SUPER
VIEWS

TO
RIGHT

↑ UP
SYCAMORE

㉓ B/W
⚲s

B/WAY
(THE DROVE)

2
COTTAGES

'NEW BARN
FARM'

KEEP ON
DOWN

'PARK
LANE'

'SHAPWKK

'BADBURY
COTTAGE'

TO S.V. WAY
AT
WHITE MILL

ROAD

1½ GATES

GOOD VIEW OF
BADBURY RINGS

3 B/W⚲s

B/WAY

9

11

HYDE
FARM

RAM LANE

QUEEN
COTTAGES

DOWN(ISH)

NEW ROAD

CRAB FARM

'PARK
LANE'

'THE
HEMSWORTH
HERD'

OVERHANGING
BEECHES

1½ GATES
BOTH SIDES

OLD CHALK
PIT

20

¼
MILE

DOWN

FROM
LEFT

DAY 2 - STAGE 11

SHAPWICK TO VINTNERS FEE

Past Piccadilly Lane on the left, the last house on the left *was* one of the last surviving village shops on our route and, in the 1st edition, I told everybody, "even if you're fully provisioned, go in and buy something - every little helps". Clearly, the tide in the affairs of man has swept this little shop away just like all the other little shops which used to be the social centre of so many villages in this country. I was very saddened to see that this last outpost had gone.

Now, there is a field on the left and more houses on the right which take you all the way into the centre of the village. Arriving at the crossroads with the Anchor Inn on the RH corner, cross over and rest awhile on the bench opposite the telephone box and the Saxon cross (the top is 1920 but the base is original) whilst I pass on some information about the lands of Shapwick. By 1268, the village had a market and a fair and its manorial lands consisted of some 3000 acres. This was substantial acreage and the Crown required an annual rent of £140 and the services of three knights for it. The Earls of Leicester were the lords of the manor at that time and they settled these knights in sub-manors of Shapwick, called the Fees. The first sub-manor, Shapwick Champagne, was named after the Earl of Leicester's knight Henry de Champagne and it had its own manor house, now Bishops Court Farm which you will soon be seeing. It is named after Archbishop Wake of Canterbury who bought it in 1750. The only other Fee of interest to this walk is Vintner's Fee, the smallest. This was given to Walter de Vynere and consisted of just twelve acres of pasture and arable which you will be traversing on your way to Crawford Bridge.

Now, walk round the corner to visit the Church of St Bartholomew. Buy a leaflet in the church for an excellent history of this parish and the church. There has been a church on this spot, near the Roman ford, since the 11thC (the Normans) and the whole of the North wall is still the original. The rest was rebuilt in 1880 but the 14thC tower was spared in a sympathetic restoration.

Returning to the Anchor Inn (completely rebuilt in 1920) at the crossroads, take the turning towards Blandford. Passing houses on right and left, you arrive at the Old School on the left and School Cottage on the right. Continue past the School and the farm buildings of Bishops Court Farm on the right after a small field. On the left, high walls protect a fine orchard, followed by Bishops Court farmhouse itself set back across a lawn with two superb copper beeches. Opposite the farmhouse, the road bends right but do not follow the road anymore. Instead, keep on straight ahead, past the 'Private Road' sign and the 'S.V.Way Crawford Bridge 1.1/4' sign. Arriving at a farm yard, stay in the yard and head for the track in the far LH corner.

Through the farmyard and past another S.V.Way arrow , follow the hedged and fenced track around a LH bend past another S.V.Way and a Footpath arrow. This bend takes you through a gap in a long, narrow coppice of beech trees and into fine, lush meadowland. On the edge of the wood, go over the farm gate and keep to the wire fence on your right for a few yards. At the S.V.Way-labelled gatepost at the end of the fence, a yellow N.T. arrow points vaguely in the direction you should take across the field but a better guide is the solitary tree in the field. Keep to the right of this tree - don't follow the tractor tracks.

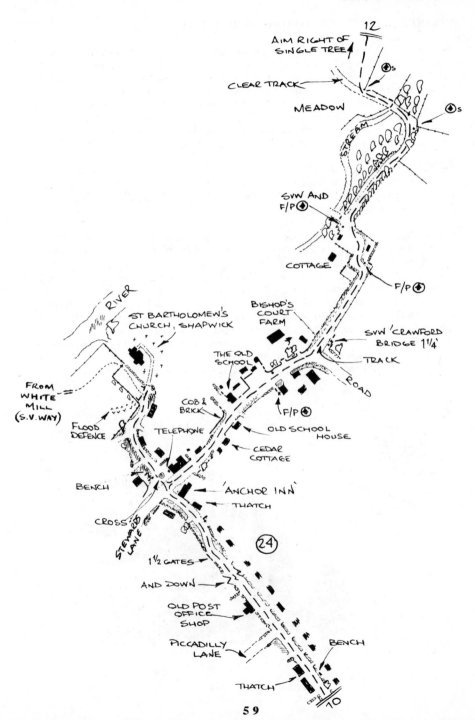

12

AIM RIGHT OF SINGLE TREE

⊕ S

CLEAR TRACK

MEADOW

⊕ S

STREAM

SVW AND F/P ⊕

COTTAGE

F/P ⊕

RIVER

ST BARTHOLOMEW'S CHURCH, SHAPWICK

BISHOP'S COURT FARM

SVW 'CRAWFORD BRIDGE 1¼'

TRACK

ROAD

THE OLD SCHOOL

FROM WHITE MILL (S.V. WAY)

FLOOD DEFENCE

COB & BRICK

TELEPHONE

F/P ⊕

OLD SCHOOL HOUSE

CEDAR COTTAGE

BENCH

'ANCHOR INN'

THATCH

CROSS

STEWARDS LANE

24

1½ GATES

AND DOWN

OLD POST OFFICE SHOP

PICCADILLY LANE

BENCH

THATCH

10

VINTNERS FEE TO CRAWFORD BRIDGE GATE

You are now in Vintner's Fee, the third sub-manor of Shapwick which derives its name from a corruption of its owner's name, Walter de Vynere. Don't go under the overhead wires in this first field - the N.T.-arrowed stile is about 70 yards right of where the wires pass over the wire fence. These are particularly long fields - about 1 mile altogether - but they're perfectly flat and easy to cross. Over the stile, maintain the same direction and this will lead you straight to the stile in the second field. You will have passed under the overhead wires in this second field and they cross over the fence about 30 yards to your right when you reach the stile.

The N.T. arrow points slightly in the wrong direction here. You need to aim 30 yards left of an electricity pole ahead of you - towards a gate in the far fence - slightly left of a 3-storey, gabled house on the hillside of Spetisbury above it in the distance - 254 degrees WSW. Can you see it alright?

On your left, the River Stour reappears before you go over the stile into the last field before Crawford Bridge - with swans, moorhens and the odd heron if you're lucky. Now, don't aim for the bridge because the way out onto the road is over the stile by a gate about 200 yards to its right. The N.T. arrow is right this time and points your way WNW 287 degrees for 1/2 mile across this last field. Eventually reaching the stile by a gate onto the road, you have a choice of Routes for Day 3 or you could visit both alternative destinations. It's quite a short Day 3 to give you chance to recover from two fairly long Days and to prepare for a longer Day 4. For now, Spetisbury village is on the other side of Crawford Bridge, so you can get your bus back to your base from there and return, refreshed, in the morning. - having decided whether to turn left and go up to Spetisbury Rings or right and visit Tarrant Crawford.

Crawford Bridge, Spetisbury

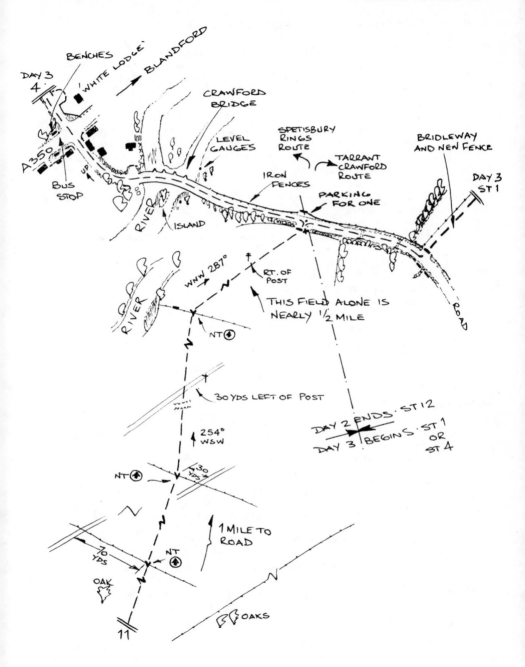

DAY 3 - INTRODUCTION

CRAWFORD BRIDGE TO BLANDFORD ST MARY

Today, you have three Options. You can visit the hill fort of Spetisbury Rings and enjoy some magnificent views of the Stour Valley, and nearly as far as the Dorset coast in the other direction, or you can pay a visit to some ancient Abbey lands and a lovely church in the valley of the River Tarrant, a tributary of the Stour.

After climbing Spetisbury Rings for the view, the first Option takes you to an abandoned Railway station where you begin an easy stroll along the railway line which has been reclaimed by shrubs, trees and birds. The others meet you at West End on the rail track and, descending from there into Charlton Marshall, you enjoy a level walk into Blandford St Mary and a visit to the market town of Blandford Forum.

The second Option is to visit the church of St Mary at Tarrant Crawford to see the 13thC and 14thC wall paintings and then walk through vineyards and across water meadows between two old mills on your way to meet the Spetisbury Rings visitors at West End for a railway stroll into Charlton Marshall and the final leg into Blandford.

Oh, yes. The third Option is to make a circular walk and visit both Spetisbury Rings and Tarrant Crawford. Start at Crawford Bridge, take the Spetisbury Option 2 and walk back along the rail track from Spetisbury Station to where you started and then follow the Tarrant Crawford Option 1. It's quite easy if you study the maps. Start where you left the stile from the Half Mile Field on the Day 2 - Stage 12 map and walk down the lane to begin Option 1 or over Crawford Bridge for Option 2 and the circuit.

STAGE		MILES	TOTAL MILES
OPTION 1:			
1	Crawford Bridge Gate to Tarrant Crawford	1	26.50
2	Tarrant Crawford to Clapcotts Farm	1.25	27.75
3	Clapcotts Farm to Charlton Marshall	1	28.75
5	Charlton Marshall to Littleton	1	29.75
6	Littleton to Blandford By-pass	1	30.75
7	Blandford By-pass to Blandford St Mary	.25	31
OPTION 2:			
4	Crawford Bridge Gate to Spetisbury Railway	1.25	26.75
3	Spetisbury Railway to Charlton Marshall	1	27.75
5 - 7	Charlton Marshall to Blandford St Mary - as Option 1	2.25	30

CRAWFORD BRIDGE TO BLANDFORD ST MARY

'Norman' barn at Tarrant Crawford

Market Square and Church of Sts Peter and Paul, Blandford Forum

DAY 3 - STAGE 1

OPTION 1 - CRAWFORD BRIDGE TO TARRANT CRAWFORD

Leaving Crawford Bridge, go back along the lane, past yesterday's stile, and keep on for 100 yards to a small gate in the LH hedge. You want to get to the power line stanchion in the far RH corner of the field. But, keeping to the new LH fence (or the edge, if the fence isn't in yet), walk straight across to a point between a high tree and the electricity pole in the opposite hedge and turn right along the hedge to the top end of the field.

On arrival in the far, top corner of the field, negotiate a complex of field and track junctions and pass under the stanchion . This junction is being relaid but head up the grass track between wire fences to exit through a cantilever gate onto a tarmac lane. Cross the lane and go through the field, uphill, to another gate onto the top road.

Across this road, go through the gate and follow the line of telegraph posts across the sloping field. Go through the next pair of gates and follow the track along the RH hedged bank and past a small quarry, to descend to the bottom of the field. The long bank at the foot of the hill between you and the farmhouse is a remnant of the precinct wall of the largest Cistercian nunnery in all England.

Straight ahead of you, you will see St Mary's Church and this is your target. Through the gate, turn left and aim for the Bridleway-arrowed gate opening onto the farm track. The foundations of the buttressed stone barn on your left date back to the 15thC when Tarrant Abbey was home to about 50 nuns. By the time abbess Margaret Russell surrendered to Henry VIII's commissioners in 1539, only 18 nuns remained, together with the lay workers who supplied and maintained the Abbey. Now, keep going right up the track to St Mary's church.

Originally dedicated to All Saints about 1170 AD, it was given by Ralph de Kahaines of Tarrant Keynston to the Anchoresses of the Manse of the Nuns which was built adjacent to the church, so it was here long before the foundation of the Abbey for the nuns in 1223. Inside St Mary's, there are the most wonderful medieval wall paintings, the earliest dating back to the 13thC. The story recounted on the South wall is the martyrdom of St Margaret of Antioch. Bishop Poore was baptised here, later becoming Bishop of Salisbury in 1217 and moving from Old Sarum to the new Cathedral. He loved Tarrant Crawford so much that he was buried in the Abbey - the coffin lid with the foliated cross on the left of the altar is believed to be his, having been moved here from the Abbey.

Leave the church by the wrought iron gate and turn right for just a few paces. Cross the river bridge and follow the LH edge of three fields with the River Tarrant on your left. When you emerge onto the tarmac driveway, follow it between the RH fence and the LH verge and trees (with another banked remnant of the old Abbey boundary) to the road again. Cross the road and go through the Footpath-arrowed gate into the vineyard. Begin to follow the LH edge with the Tarrant behind the trees.

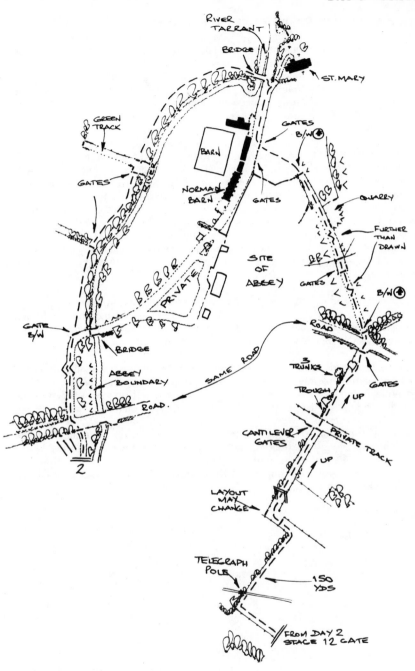

RIVER TARRANT

BRIDGE

ST. MARY

GREEN TRACK

GATES B/W

BARN

GATES

GATES

QUARRY

NORMAN BARN

GATES

FURTHER THAN DRAWN

B/W

PRIVATE

SITE OF ABBEY

GATES

B/W

GATE B/W

BRIDGE

ROAD

3 TRUNKS

ABBEY BOUNDARY

SAME ROAD

TROUGH

UP

GATES

ROAD

CANTILEVER GATES

PRIVATE TRACK

UP

2

LAYOUT MAY CHANGE

TELEGRAPH POLE

150 YDS

FROM DAY 2 STAGE 12 GATE

65

TARRANT CRAWFORD TO CLAPCOTTS FARM

Follow the green track along the bottom edge of the vineyard, down to the 'Picnic Area' in the far LH corner.   Behind the hedge, the Tarrant joins the first part of the divided River Stour.   Bearing right, follow the track along, through a row of poplars and through a field of soft fruit bushes.   With a wood-fenced paddock down on your left, follow the track and you will emerge onto a gravel track with a car park for 'Pick-Your-Own' produce and a farm shop opposite.   This could be a good chance to replenish your stocks of fruit for this relatively short Day.

Anyway, turn left down the track, passing a ford into the river on your left and a house with adorning wisteria on your immediate right.   Follow the narrowing path to cross the first part of the River Stour by a pedestrian bridge made from old iron rail track and concrete.   Mind your head on a very low, overhanging branch.   Natural meanderings and man-made diversions have divided the Stour into several sections across this wide meadow.   One part serves Keynston Mill where you are now whilst another main part (about 1/3 mile away) serves the defunct Clapcott Mill.   A third equal part flows straight through the middle of the plain and a smaller central section is no more than a boggy ditch which dries up completely in anything but the wettest weather.

Across the railed bridge, keep straight on across the meadow and over a sleeper bridge across the dried up ditch.   Again, keep straight on to another handrailed, rail track and concrete bridge with new trees on both banks of the Stour.   Keep straight on again with a view of Spetisbury Rings over on your front left.

Arriving at the far side of the wide floodplain/meadow, go through a small gate onto a meandering, narrow path with nettles and scrub either side.   This path comes out onto a bridge over sluice gates serving the old mill.   The mill is now a superb home on your left and the garages on your right have accommodation above.

Follow the Footpath arrows quickly right/left across the gravel drive and take the Footpath-arrowed, long footbridge which begins next to the drive through the lovely private gardens.   I know it's tempting to stand and stare, but try not to intrude too much on the privacy of the occupiers.   Keep walking along the bridge above the superbly landscaped gardens.

3

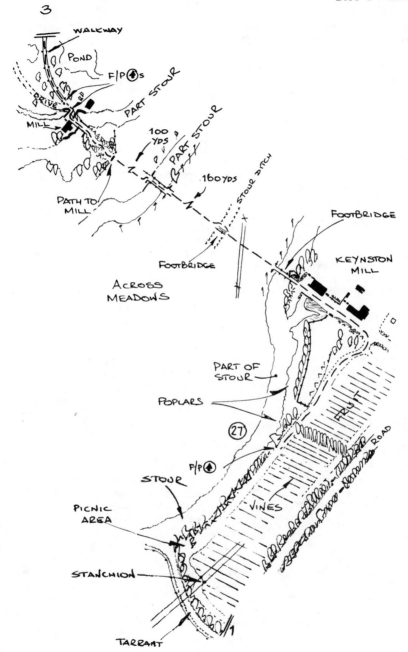

WALKWAY

POND

F/P④s

PART STOUR

DRIVE

MILL

PART STOUR

100 YDS

PART STOUR

PATH TO MILL

160 YDS

STOUR DITCH

FOOTBRIDGE

KEYNSTON MILL

ACROSS MEADOWS

FOOTBRIDGE

PART OF STOUR

POPLARS

㉗

F/P④

STOUR

ROAD

PICNIC AREA

VINES

STANCHION

TARRANT

1

DAY 3 - STAGE 3

CLAPCOTTS FARM TO CHARLTON MARSHALL OR SPETISBURY RAILWAY TO CHARLTON MARSHALL

OPTION 1 - FROM KEYNSTON MILL:
Keep going along the footbridge until it crosses a diverted tributary of the Stour which provides water and a stream for the garden pools. Then, after passing between the end of a brick wall and a garage, join the gravel drive from the old mill as it passes between a LH fenced field and the barns and farm cottages of Clapcotts Farm over on your right.

At the end of the drive, you emerge onto the A350 Blandford road with a Footpath sign pointing back to 'Keynston Mill' and a stream running under the road to flow parallel to the LH hedge back to the Stour.

Cross over the main road - carefully, now - and pass the school grounds on your left as you wander up to the railway bridge which crosses the road. Just before the bridge at West End, go through the gate, onto the rising, wood-railed 'Public Footpath'. This Permissive Path takes you up onto the track of the old Blandford to Poole railway line which disappeared during the 'Beeching cuts' in the 1960s. Arriving on top, turn sharp right and follow the path along the track with thin beeches and sycamores growing in the embankments - along with encroaching brambles, hawthorns and allsorts. Or - if you want to see Spetisbury Rings as well, turn left and follow the track to the abandoned Spetisbury Station. Then turn off onto the Stage 4 map.

OPTION 2 - FROM SPETISBURY RINGS:
You are now in a very deep cutting, with the RH embankment being much steeper and higher than the left. Then the track emerges onto an embankment with a field on your left and the big 'Copper Beech House' and Spetisbury Church down on your right. In a few steps, a Permissive Path sign on your right indicates a path where those who took the Keynston Mill route are coming up past Spetisbury First School to join you for the last stages into Blandford.

ALL TOGETHER NOW:
After the track crosses the bridge above the road at West End, there are spring-fed watercress beds down on your left. The path opens and narrows as it progresses along the rail track and, slightly uppish, it passes a wood of firs up on your left before a deep cutting carries it under a concrete footbridge. After that, the track is elevated above gardens and houses down on your right and a field on your left.

Immediately after that, a set of steps on the right runs down to an open area before a small housing estate on the edge of Charlton Marshall. Go past these steps and take the wider ramp which takes you down to an exit stile and a horse-step onto a grassy play area and a wood-fenced childs' playground.

Everybody turn to Stage 5

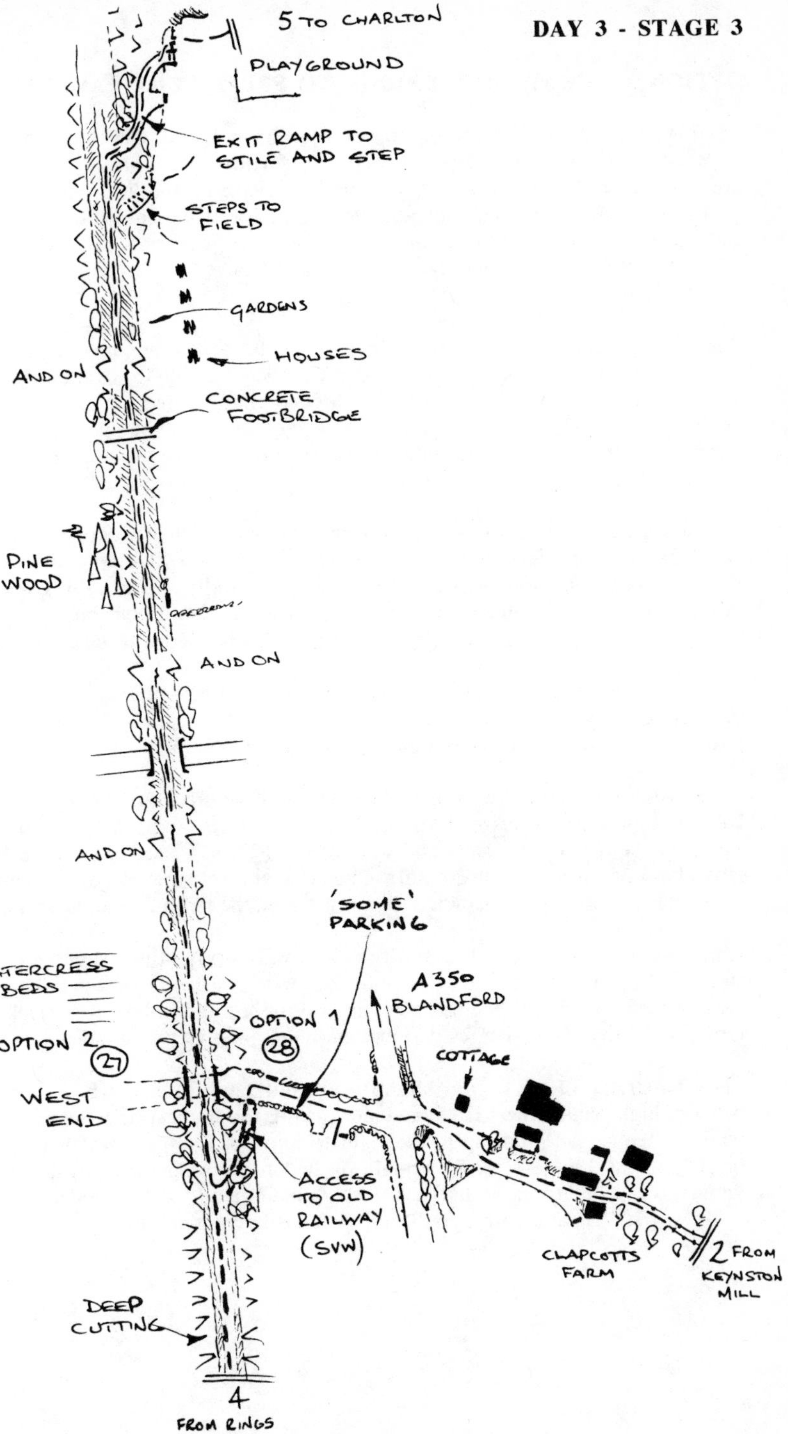

5 TO CHARLTON

DAY 3 - STAGE 3

PLAYGROUND

EXIT RAMP TO
STILE AND STEP

STEPS TO
FIELD

GARDENS

HOUSES

AND ON

CONCRETE
FOOTBRIDGE

PINE
WOOD

AND ON

AND ON

'SOME'
PARKING

A 350
BLANDFORD

WATERCRESS
BEDS

OPTION 1

COTTAGE

OPTION 2
(27)

(28)

WEST
END

ACCESS
TO OLD
RAILWAY
(SVW)

CLAPCOTTS
FARM

2 FROM
KEYNSTON
MILL

DEEP
CUTTING

4
FROM RINGS

69

DAY 3 - STAGE 4

OPTION 2 - CRAWFORD BRIDGE TO SPETISBURY RAILWAY

Leaving Crawford Bridge, keep going up the hill and, very carefully, cross over the A350 Blandford road at Spetisbury where you will find a bench and a bus stop (you probably found it yesterday, but never mind). Walk up the hill opposite, known as 'Louse Lane' for some imponderable reason, and past the entrances to White Lodge and Eagles. After the remnants of the rail bridge, turn right and go over the Footpath-arrowed stile into the elevating field next to the railway embankment. *Don't take the path up to the Railway track.*

Walk up the field, close to the wire fence and, in the top corner, go over the stile into a mixed pine and deciduous wood. Wend your way through the overhanging branches and leave by a similar gap or stile into a deep chalky ditch. This is part of the Spetisbury Ring embankment and a very steep climb takes you up onto the top. So, scramble up it and turn left to follow the Footpath along the top - or turn left and find the easier path up to the top of the ring.

As you wander carefully along the top ring, the views will provoke you into looking all around but wait until you reach the O.S. trig point so that you can look safely. You can make out Charborough Park tower, the radio masts at Rampisham, the Purbeck hills and the Blandford Army Camp tower. With your binoculars and O.S. map, you could spend ages up here discovering places at great distances all around.

Anyway, time beckons, so keep walking around the rim of the inner ring - rather undulating, so be careful - until you reach the opening in the banks which leads you into the LH field. Cross the field to the gate on the other side.

Go through the gate in the hedge where you will find a Footpath signpost pointing back to 'Spetisbury Rings and Middle Buildings 3/4'. With a huge old tree facing you over the hedge, turn right and walk down the road, past a big lime tree and a laburnum just before a Footpath-arrowed gate on the left which leads to a path above a huge, cob-walled kitchen garden. In a few yards, the rail bridge crosses this road.

Don't go under the bridge but turn right and walk up the three flights of grey-brick steps to the top where you will find the twin platforms of Spetisbury Station. Double back round and begin a pleasant walk along the old railway track, instantly crossing the road you have just left and enjoying good views on either side.

The first stretch of track goes slightly downhill and, after a while, the path runs between high banks, the LH embankment being the highest and steepest. After a while, a stepped path runs up to the right to join the Footpath which goes overhead on the railway bridge. Keep straight on under the bridge and turn to Stage 3. I know it seems odd to be going back a Stage but I had to accommodate the Option 1 walkers first. Don't worry, you'll follow it easily enough when you see the Stage 3 details.

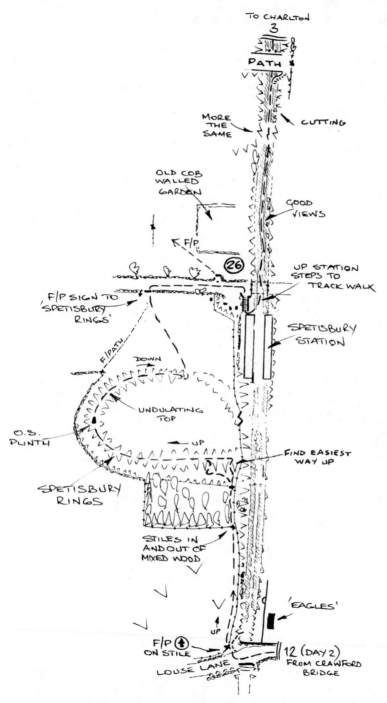

TO CHARLTON
3

PATH

MORE
THE
SAME

CUTTING

OLD COB
WALLED
GARDEN

GOOD
VIEWS

F/P

26

UP STATION
STEPS TO
TRACK WALK

F/P SIGN TO
'SPETISBURY
RINGS'

SPETISBURY
STATION

F/PATH

DOWN

UNDULATING
TOP

O.S.
PLINTH

UP

FIND EASIEST
WAY UP

SPETISBURY
RINGS

STILES IN
AND OUT OF
MIXED WOOD

'EAGLES'

F/P
ON STILE

UP

12 (DAY 2)
FROM CRAWFORD
BRIDGE

LOUSE LANE

CHARLTON MARSHALL TO LITTLETON

Follow the road past the fenced Playground and wander down through Hopegood Close, turning left at the T-junction. At the instant crossroad, with the hedged lane turning up to your left to pass under the Railway line you have just left and with Charlton Mead opposite, turn right into The Close and walk downhill. On the RH side of the road, near the foot of the hill, there is the village pump with the date 1887 opposite the 'Antiques' store. There is a Post Office on the RH corner and a bus stop on its far side. Possibly pausing at the bench on the LH corner green or walking right down the A350 for a quick lemonade at The Charlton Inn, come back here and continue along the main road to the left.

For added security, cross over to the RH side of the road and follow the service road pavement alongside the iron-railed field. At the end of the field, a wide track takes the signed Bridleway down to ford the Stour at what used to be the arrival point into Charlton Marshall in the 1st edition. Aren't you glad you don't have to go through the depth-sounding, paddling and drying routine any more?

Go through the gate on the corner to pay a short visit to the Church of St Mary the Virgin. Except for the base of the tower, the church was rebuilt in 1713 by Thomas Bastard, whose sons were later to rebuild Blandford Forum after the disastrous fire of 1731. It is considered to be the best example of Georgian design outside London. It has a tall, canopied pulpit, a font similar to that in Blandford's church of Saints Peter and Paul, clear windows and numerous memorials. Outside, note the fine stone and flint walls and the double-fronted sundial over the porch.

Church Lane opposite is the continuation of the Roman Road from Buzbury Rings and leads up to Charlton Down and on to Maiden Castle, the major hill fort just outside Dorchester. Continue along the main road and, after a stretch of wooden fencing on both sides of the A350 and a small development of converted farm buildings on the right, opposite Old Wayside House on the LH side of the road, turn down Gravel Lane.

On the LH side of this lane, is the fine thatched, stone-mullioned Old Dairy Cottage whilst, on the LH bend, the road comes very close to the Stour and there are two more benches where you may pass a few idle moments. Then keep straight on, between old cottages, the odd huge chestnuts and a couple of small fields until the road disappears into a 'Private' gravel-surfaced area near Little Manor Cottages on your right. By some large chestnut trees on your left, go through the Footpath-arrowed, staggered iron barrier into a narrow, hedged and iron-fenced path.

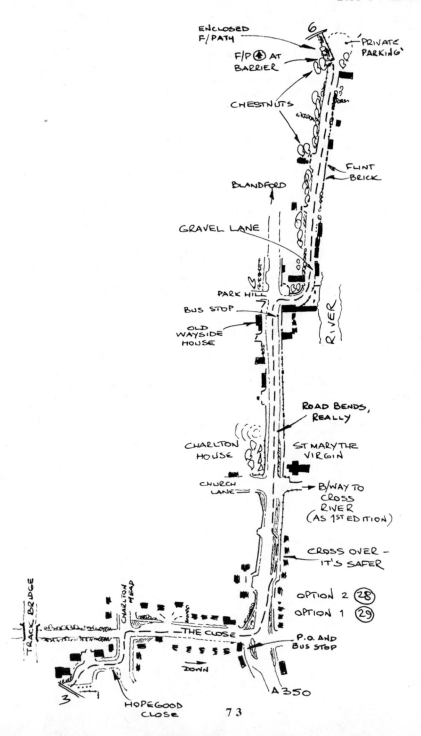

ENCLOSED F/PATH

F/P ⊕ AT BARRIER

'PRIVATE PARKING'

CHESTNUTS

FLINT BRICK

BLANDFORD

GRAVEL LANE

PARK HILL

BUS STOP

OLD WAYSIDE HOUSE

RIVER

ROAD BENDS, REALLY

CHARLTON HOUSE

ST MARY THE VIRGIN

CHURCH LANE

B/WAY TO CROSS RIVER (AS 1ST EDITION)

CROSS OVER — IT'S SAFER

OPTION 2 ㉘
OPTION 1 ㉙

P.O. AND BUS STOP

TRACK BRIDGE

CHARLTON MEAD

THE CLOSE

DOWN

HOPEGOOD CLOSE

A350

3

DAY 3 - STAGE 6

LITTLETON TO BLANDFORD BY-PASS

Now, with a hedged field on your left and an iron fence on your right, follow this path into an overgrown hollow-way where a stile leads you onto - and straight across - a Private driveway. Over the opposite stile with the Footpath arrow, aim diagonally left, well to the left of the first huge oak tree in this field and towards the large Georgian house standing on the A350 - WNW 292 degrees to be precise.

Keeping in line with the Georgian house, you arrive at a stile with a Footpath arrow at the end of the hedge by a pair of farm gates. Over the A350, is a Bridleway and the entrance to Littleton Farm alongside a high, buttressed brick wall. Carefully cross the road to the pavement and follow the wall which borders the Georgian house.

Look out for the wicked draught from the passing heavy lorries and press on towards Blandford St Mary, the sign for which is soon passed after a banked hedge and wooden fence bounding Orchard House on your left. You will have passed a couple of houses on your right backing onto open fields and, after the next two houses, a 6ft wooden fence follows round the next corner of the lane leading right down to Lower Blandford St Mary only, past some converted barns and a church. However, keep straight on, with the traffic, past a Footpath and Bridleway sign pointing uphill to your left, a postbox in the wall on the other side of the road and the Moose Hall where the road comes back out from Lower Blandford St Mary.

You will soon be free of all this traffic as, just ahead, you pass the road direction sign before the Blandford By-Pass. Most traffic turns onto the By-Pass and leaves you to wander down Upton Lane opposite into Blandford St Mary. Across the By-Pass, keep to the LH pavement, past the electricity sub-station. Over on your right lies the vast Tesco Supermarket - That sort of thing doesn't help little Shapwick-type shops one iota.

Anyway, negotiate the next island and pass the bus stop en route for the end of today's walk.

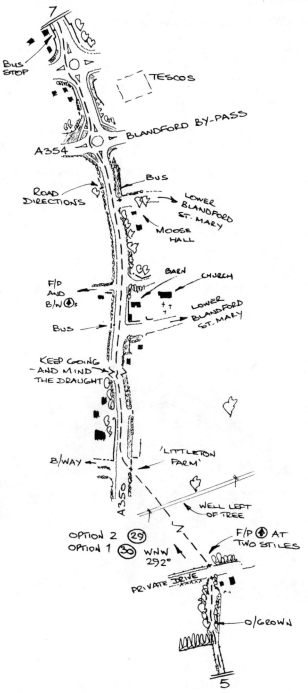

7

BUS
STOP

TESCOS

BLANDFORD BY-PASS

A354

BUS

ROAD
DIRECTIONS

LOWER
BLANDFORD
ST. MARY

MOOSE
HALL

BARN

CHURCH

F/D
AND
B/W ⓦs

LOWER
BLANDFORD
ST. MARY

BUS

KEEP GOING
- AND MIND
THE DRAUGHT

B/WAY

'LITTLETON
FARM'

A350

WELL LEFT
OF TREE

OPTION 2 ㉙
OPTION 1 ㉚   WNW
292°

F/P ⓟ AT
TWO STILES

PRIVATE DRIVE

O/GROWN

5

75

DAY 3 - STAGE 7

BLANDFORD BY-PASS TO BLANDFORD ST MARY

Keep straight on, with the Old School, the sports field and the Hall and Woodhouse Brewery - Est. 1778 'Badger Beers' - all on your right and with several small housing areas on your left.   Towards the end of the road, take special note of the red and grey brick Brook House on your left and also the brick and flint wall on the other side of the road.   These combinations of building materials typify the style of rebuilding by the Bastard brothers after the terrible fire of June 1731.   The centre of Blandford Forum today is the most complete and cohesive surviving example of a Georgian town in all England.   This walk really does seem to be encompassed by superlatives.

If you came via Tarrant Crawford, you will have done 1 mile more than the Spetisbury Rings visitors but, if you did the complete circle through Tarrant Crawford and Spetisbury Rings and walked the whole length of the railway from Louse Lane to Charlton Marshall to complete the circuit, you will have done 2.1/2 miles more.   To simplify matters, the mileages shown from Blandford St Mary onwards will all be the shorter total and you'll have to add your extras to the total at the end when you're telling your friends how far you have walked.   Sorry.

A walk into Blandford Forum is now called for so, if you turn right and cross the River Stour bridge you can go and explore or get a cup of tea (or something stronger) and have a nice relaxing end to Day 3.

Bryanston School Lodge, Blandford St Mary

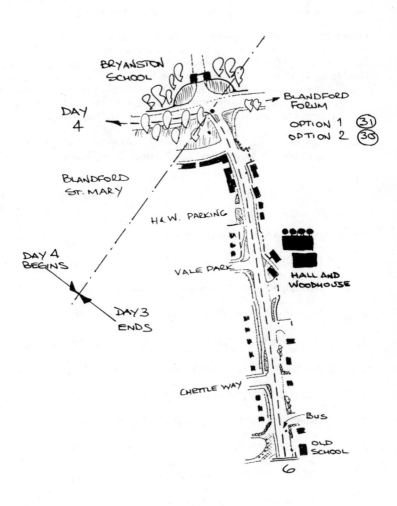

DAY 4 - INTRODUCTION

BLANDFORD ST MARY TO STURMINSTER NEWTON

You'll need to be a little fitter for this Stage as you have some gradients to tackle. Nothing horrendous, but our path goes over Hambledon Hill fort in the middle of the Day for some magnificent views over the Stour Valley.   If you don't really fancy the climb when you get there, a level country lane option is offered.

Before then, the path wanders through the Portman family's Estate of Bryanston and through the riverside village of Durweston for another mill and a few ghost stories. The village of Stourpaine comes next and, after the hillforts of Hod Hill and Hambledon Hill (with a tremendous high-level stroll) the route continues through Child Okeford, nestling serenely at the foot of Hambledon Hill.   After the physical excesses of the hill fort, easier walking through level countryside leads to a fine, thatched manor house at Hammoon and yet another mill at Fiddleford.

The last easy mile leads you to Sturminster Newton, the 'capital' of the Blackmore Vale (Thomas Hardy's Vale of the Little Dairies), to end a most satisfying Day.

	STAGE	MILES	TOTAL MILES
1	Blandford St Mary to Bryanston	1.25	31.25
2	Bryanston to Bryanston School	.50	31.75
3	Bryanston School to Bryanston Drive	.50	32.25
4	Bryanston Drive to Durweston	.50	32.75
5	Durweston to Stourpaine	.50	33.25
6	Stourpaine to Child Okeford Road	1	34.25
7	Child Okeford Road to Hambledon Hill	.50	34.75
8	Hambledon Hill to Child Okeford	1	35.75
9	Through Child Okeford	.50	36.25
10	Child Okeford to Newmans Drove	.75	37
11	Newmans Drove to Stour Fields	1	38
12	Stour Fields through Hammoon	1	39
13	Hammoon to Fiddleford Mill	1	40
14	Fiddleford Mill to Penny Street	.75	40.75
15	Penny Street to Sturminster Newton	.25	41

BLANDFORD ST MARY TO STURMINSTER NEWTON

Top:
Holy Trinity Church and
lychgate, Stourpaine

Bottom:
St Nicholas' Church,
Child Okeford

DAY 4 - STAGE 1

BLANDFORD ST MARY TO BRYANSTON

Now, back where you arrived on Day 3, outside the large stone entrance Lodge to Bryanston School, walk straight on along the old Blandford-Dorchester road between the tree-bedecked green and the low stone-wall of Bryanston School grounds.   Over the green, in the side road, you will see the 'Stour Inn', strangely the only inn with this name on the entire route.   Go past the columned porch of Berkeley Lodge and on to the first turning on your right, New Road, signposted to 'Bryanston 1.1/4'.

The old main road now continues to a dead end because of the new By-Pass whilst, between this and New Road, the centre route goes off into the country to Winterborne Stickland.   In New Road, pass between rows of brick cottages on either side of the road and past a Footpath-signed gateway which leads into the fields of the open valley on your left.   Past The Old Riding School on your right, start a mile long tarmac, uphill walk.   The long, ivy-clad flint and brick wall on your right is the boundary wall of the Bryanston Estate beyond which a mixed wood of mainly beeches, oaks, sycamores and pines is thriving. .

Keep on uphill, passing the solitary old chestnut in the hedge on your left where you can enjoy the views across the wide and open valley.   Continuing uphill, with fine views on your left, you may fancy a rest.   On your right, you will find a commemorative seat from Queen Elizabeth's Silver Jubilee in 1977 and a similar memorial seat a little further on.   As this is quite a long hill, a short rest may be permitted whilst I tell you something of the estate's history.

In the Domesday Book of 1087, a 2500 acre estate was owned by Bryan de l'Isle (He came from the Isle of Wight).   He gave his name to Bryan's-ton, meaning town or settlement.   The estate passed through many hands until the 1680s when it was sold to Sir William Berkeley-Portman.   His family kept it until 1927 when death duties of the last Lord Portman caused the estate and the new house, which was only completed in 1897, to pass to the Crown Commissioners.   The first Bryanston House, in medieval manor style, stood down near the River Stour (where the church still exists on private land) but this was replaced in 1778 by a fashionable, classical-style country seat by the architect James Wyatt.   This later house apparently suffered terrible damp problems throughout its life and it was finally demolished in favour of the current Bryanston House, on drier ground on top of the hill.   Only the gate-house which you saw earlier today remains from the James Wyatt era.

Anyway, nearing the top of *this* hill, after a gate and three single trees on your left, you arrive at a turning on the right which is signposted 'Bryanston' and 'Bryanston School 1/2'.

The signpost confirms that this is the old Cliff Lodge entrance to the estate and, following the estate road into 'Forum View', you will be amongst houses and scattered cottages for the next 1/4 mile.   Keep to the road as it zig-zags left and right past the low flint garden wall of the older cottages on your left and past 'The Cliff' sign on the next RH bend.

After a couple of red-brick houses and the yard of a garage/workshop on the left and a service road on your right, just keep straight on and look out for the telephone box ahead.

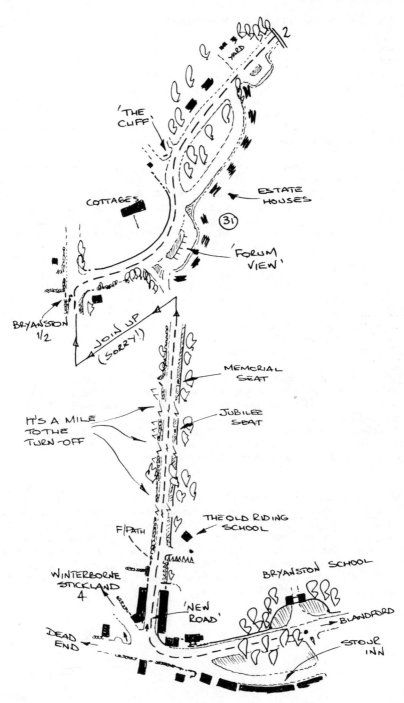

'THE CLIFF'

COTTAGES

ESTATE HOUSES

(31)

'FORUM VIEW'

BRYANSTON ½

JOIN UP (SORRY!)

MEMORIAL SEAT

IT'S A MILE TO THE TURN-OFF

JUBILEE SEAT

THE OLD RIDING SCHOOL

F/PATH

WINTERBORNE STICKLAND 4

BRYANSTON SCHOOL

'NEW ROAD'

BLANDFORD

DEAD END

STOUR INN

DAY 4 - STAGE 2

BRYANSTON TO BRYANSTON SCHOOL

Go through the arrowless kissing gate next to the 'phone box and walk diagonally right down the field of Park-style trees, passing under the telephone wires and brushing against the RH side of a rather poorly chestnut tree. Aim for the LH end of the red brick building in the dip ahead of you. This line leads you to a second kissing gate in the iron and wire fence at the far side of the field. Through the gate, you emerge into the wide car park between outbuildings of the Bryanston Village and Estate Club. The road you left at the telephone box emerges onto your route from the far RH corner of the Club and then turns into the village, rejoining your path.

Passing a row of arched stables on your left and three trees on the village green on your right, you come to Bryanston Stores and Post Office at the end of the row of cottages. Just after this, a track to Home Farm goes up on your left, to the side of an amazing collection of old horse shoes fixed to the wall of the cottage in the next garden. Over the low flint garden wall on your right, there is a small orchard whilst a similar low wall goes round the opposite, left corner towards the yards of Home Farm and Nos. 12-18 Portman Mews.

Turn right at the T-junction, following the main estate road but only for a few steps to the next road which comes uphill from sharp left. Follow the banked, walled verge around the LH hairpin and cross to the RH hedge over which a farmyard full of large barns is busy below you in the dip. Ahead, the road now divides with the main route turning uphill between bramble covered iron fences. A track straight ahead of you leads past an open-fronted farm equipment shelter into fields whilst another track descends to your right into the farmyard.

Turn down this right turning as if going to the yard but don't go all the way in. Keep straight on, with the fence on your left, towards the front of the farmhouse on your right. Go through the kissing gate which faces the farmhouse and turn instantly right to follow the line of the fence (342 degrees - nearly due North) up the grassy slopes of the field on the other side. Passing about 80 yards to the right of a single large tree on the hillside, go over another stile (still no Footpath arrows) and keep to the same 342 degrees direction for another 150 yards towards a kissing gate in the top RH corner ahead of you.

As you approach Bryanston School, let me tell you a story. In the earlier James Wyatt house, during the final illness of Edward Berkeley Portman, (the 1st Viscount Portman, whose son William built the present House), an old nurse often heard someone walking about and talking in his Lordship's room in the dead of night. She went in twice but, both times, found that he was fast asleep. Being asked about it the next morning, Lord Portman did not seem at all surprised and replied, "Oh, that often happens, it's nothing to hurt". After the old House was demolished, the ghost was often seen wandering about the empty site.

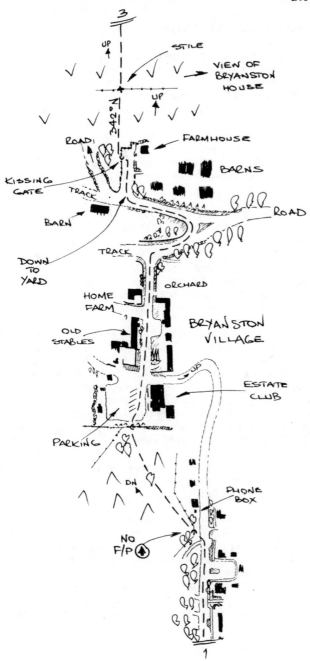

DAY 4 - STAGE 3

BRYANSTON SCHOOL TO BRYANSTON DRIVE

On arrival at the kissing gate, keep to exactly the same direction on the other side, following an imaginary line straight ahead.   Don't bother checking your compass until you're clear of the gate as the iron seems to adversely affect the magnetic field. Opposite you, the school road turns off before forming a loop which serves another brick building.   Go into the first part of the branch road but *don't go round the loop.* Your imaginary line will lead you across slightly uphill lawns, past the LH end of a long, red-brick building, to zig-zag rt/lt around a small wood and regain your original direction.   Here, you will find a narrow, cut grass path with bushes on your left and a drop down the right embankment to some modern, green sports halls belonging to the School.   The Public Footpath may not be signposted just here but it is quite easy to follow.

Follow the path on the edge of the bank around three sides of the green, corrugated school halls in the hollow, following a fenced field on your left and descending to a stile in the bottom LH corner.   At the Footpath-arrowed stile, turn right and follow the level path alongside a RH bank and a LH mixed wood of beeches and pines.   Keep to the path, past a Footpath arrow and a School sign in stylised writing 'Public Footpath'.   Just past this sign, where the path divides straight on or down a sudden left hairpin, take the sudden left hairpin and begin a steep descent into a dense wood known as 'The Hanging' - the common name for a beech wood on the edge of a scarp.

The James Wyatt house was demolished before the completion of the present house and, when an old woman was heard to say, "Ha, the Portmans won't have any luck now they've taken the roof off a ghost", this was popularly believed - and the family's misfortune was predicted another way as well.   Flocks of white and coloured peacocks lived on the estate, "having eyes on their tail feathers which resembled watermarks on writing paper".   It was said that, if the peacocks left Bryanston, the Portmans would soon follow.   Predictably, after the 2nd Viscount died in 1919, the 3rd Viscount disposed of the peacocks and, as we have heard, the House and part of the estate was sold in 1927 to pay his father's death duties.

Whilst recalling matters ghostly - especially as you are now in the rustling woods - there is talk around Bryanston of a ghostly pack of Portman Hunt hounds, one of whom is exceptionally large - and headless.

Keep on down the steep track, between pines and beech trees, to the bottom where the track divides at a laurel-clad junction.   Take the right track down to the road, emerging by a backward-pointing Footpath arrow.   Turn left, with the Stour down the bank on your right and with fine beeches, sycamores and copper beeches alongside the road.   Keep straight on and follow the tarmac road out past Middle Lodge.   With the LH field spreading uphill to a wood and the RH meadow flowing away to the Stour and towards Durweston bridge and the A350, keep straight on. Soon, a Footpath signpost by a LH gate confirms that you have come 1 mile from Bryanston.

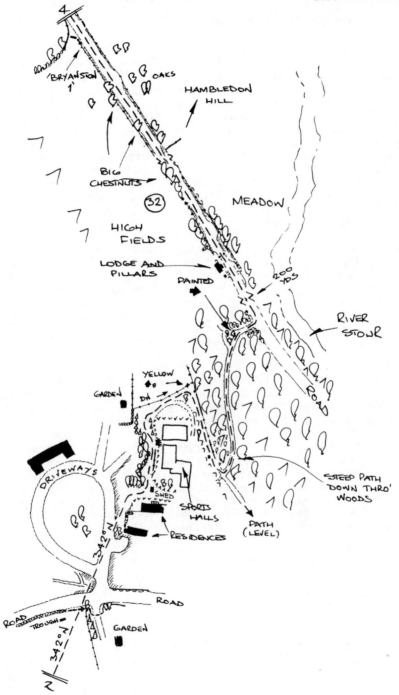

DAY 4 - STAGE 4

BRYANSTON DRIVE TO DURWESTON

Before you leave the Portman/Bryanston School estate road, there is just one more tale which is worth recounting. In the old house in 1870, a new maid who lived-in was awakened one night by an old lady who came into her room, stood and stared at her for a while and then went out again. In the morning, the new maid asked the housekeeper who the lady was but the housekeeper didn't know because they had no house visitors at the time. Later the same day, the maid was being shown around the house by the housekeeper when she saw a picture hanging on the wall. Pointing at it, she said, "That's the lady who came into my room last night". Taken aback, the housekeeper told the maid, "That's Aunt Charlotte. She's been dead for years".

Anyway, keep straight on, past the high-banked, fenced field on your left, the Old Dairy Farm House on your right and the LH turning to Knighton House School. A little further on your right, there is a section of pavement running from Durweston School's playing field as far as the church.

After the LH turn into Haycombe and 'to the Glebe', you will see the old B R Station sign for 'Stourpaine and Durweston Halt' screwed to the playground wall. Later today, you will pass through Stourpaine and walk along part of the old track on its way to Sturminster Newton. Past the Old School and the New First School on your right and a row of thatched cottages on your left, you arrive at St Nicholas' Church. The church was largely rebuilt in 1847 by P C Hardwick but it retains the strange sculpture of St Eloy shoeing a horse by taking its leg off for ease of working. The knight who presumably owns the horse is holding it up so that it doesn't fall over - being partially legless.

Past the church and Knighton House on your right and a fine brick and flint house and the entrance to 'The Old Rectory' on your left, you reach a T-junction. Turn right and go down the hill, between rows of cottages, some brick sheds and past the telephone box, towards the main A357 at the foot of the hill - Durweston Cross.

The signpost points back up the hill to 'Bryanston 4.1/4' but that is the distance all around the perimeter of the School grounds on public roads. Turn left, crossing the road to the pavement opposite. Walk along past a garage and the war memorial over on your left and past a bus shelter and another Jubilee bench against the field fence on your right. Turn down the first wide gravel track on your right, signed 'Public Bridleway and Jubilee Trail'. After a 'Private Road' notice, keep following the track for another 150 yards into the gravel yard of Durweston Mill.

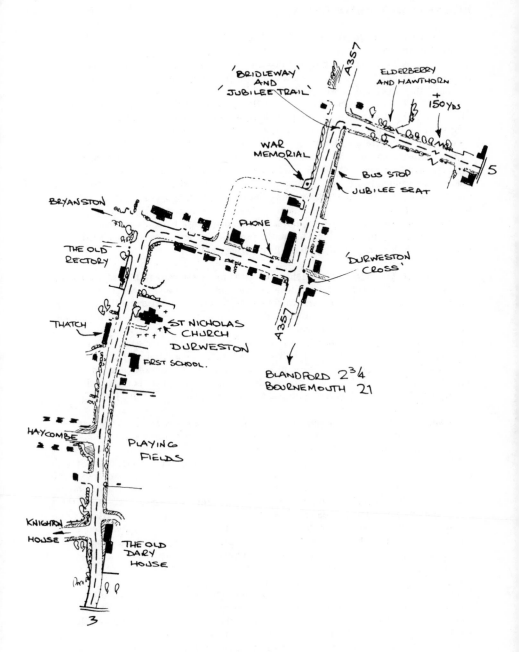

'BRIDLEWAY'
AND
'JUBILEE TRAIL'

A357

ELDERBERRY
AND HAWTHORN

+ 150 YDS

5

WAR
MEMORIAL

BUS STOP

JUBILEE SEAT

BRYANSTON

PHONE

'DURWESTON
CROSS'

THE OLD
RECTORY

THATCH

ST NICHOLAS
CHURCH
DURWESTON

A357

FIRST SCHOOL.

BLANDFORD 2¾4
BOURNEMOUTH 21

HAYCOMBE

PLAYING
FIELDS

KNIGHTON
HOUSE

THE OLD
DAIRY
HOUSE

3

DURWESTON TO STOURPAINE

Walk to the end of Durweston Mill yard to a pair of iron gates marked 'Private. Durweston Angling Club Only'.   Turn left to at a notice which reads 'Deo Benedictus Sis' and cross over the iron-railed sluice gate bridge by the mill race.   The river rushes into the deep pool on your right from the more placid headwaters of the branch on your left.   Keep on, between railings and hedges, to a half gate which leads onto a riverside field.   Bear right, ignoring the left path which follows the riverside, and go over or round a drainage pipe which leads from this field directly into the river on your right.   Arriving at the gated, concrete and iron footbridge, cross the main river onto a narrow concrete path with a field fence on your left.   Until the wider track which shares your direction goes under the old railway embankment ahead, this concrete path keeps you out of the mud until you reach the other side of the bridge - unless it's particularly wet and the mud etc. has flowed over it.   Never mind, out on the other side, turn off the track by going through a kissing gate on your left into the field alongside the railway embankment.   Follow the grassy path, bearing slightly away from the embankment, through traces of an earthwork bank across your path, to a stile in the wire fence ahead.   This fence runs along the top of another earthwork, both of which meet against the top hedge on your right.

This stile leads you into another field with barns away on your right and a fence on your left which you follow to a stile and gate onto the road by the Holy Trinity Church, Stourpaine.   The first known church built here was between 1190 and 1300 but it was rebuilt in the 15thC.   It was sadly dilapidated by 1842 and T H Wyatt was called in to design a new building in 1855.   The flint and stone church was finished and re-consecrated on 6th April 1858 in the original Perpendicular style.   It retained the original 15thC West tower and the kneeling Puritan vicar figure of John Straight of the late 17thC.   There is a fine scrap-book inside the church for your enjoyment and information and, whilst you are inside, notice the contrast between the crisp stonework of the Wyatt building with the rough greensand stone of the 15thC tower.

Stourpaine has existed as a village since Saxon times and was known as *Stures* from 'Stour'.   The original lords of the manor were the Paynes and the manor was called *Stures Payn*, changing along the way to *'Stoures Payne'* and finally in 1629 to Stourpaine.   During the dark days of the General Enclosure Act of 1801, coupled with the price rises consequent upon the Napoleonic Wars, Stourpaine suffered extreme poverty.   Open fields and common pastures were divided into smaller, uneconomic (for the tenants) fields.   Some copyholding tenants who could not find their documents (which usually dated back to earlier generations) lost their land completely.   Pasture land brought bigger profits for the landowners and needed less labourers than did arable farming.   All in all, the words of the rustic John Clare's 1793 poem must have rung painfully true around here: *"Inclosure, thou'rt a curse upon the land,   And tasteless was the wretch who thy existence plann'd"*.

Keep straight on, past the Old School on your right and Manor Farm and several cottages on your left.   Now, briefly, you have to decide whether to take the high dry road over HOD HILL or the low (muddier in its later stages) road around it by the RIVER STOUR.   For the high road, keep straight on along Manor Road.   For the low road, take the first left into Havelins and carry on, past houses to right and left, until the road goes over a stream and becomes a track.   A Bridleway sign to 'Hanford' points to the right along Hod Drive track, past a couple of thatched, flint cottages.

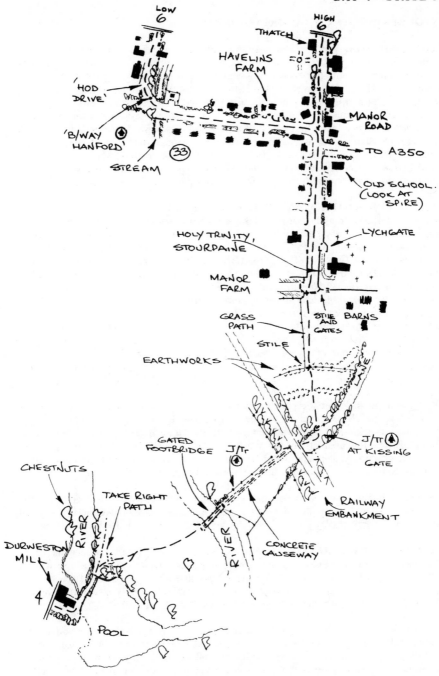

LOW
6

THATCH

HIGH
6

HAVELINS
FARM

'HOD
DRIVE'

MANOR
ROAD

'B/WAY
HANFORD'

TO A350

STREAM

33

OLD SCHOOL.
(LOOK AT
SPIRE)

HOLY TRINITY,
STOURPAINE

LYCHGATE

MANOR
FARM

STILE
AND
GATES

BARNS

GRASS
PATH

STILE

EARTHWORKS

GATED
FOOTBRIDGE

J/Tr

J/Tr
AT KISSING
GATE

CHESTNUTS

TAKE RIGHT
PATH

RIVER

RIVER

RAILWAY
EMBANKMENT

DURWESTON
MILL

CONCRETE
CAUSEWAY

4

POOL

DAY 4 - STAGE 6

STOURPAINE TO CHILD OKEFORD ROAD

THE HOD HILL WAY - Follow Manor Road until it becomes a streamside path. Follow the stream, meandering to the opposite bank, until its emergence from the RH field. Walk slowly up the steep hollow-way all the way to the gate with the N.T. sign leading onto the banked rings of Hod Hill. Follow the winding, well-trodden grass track through the rings and up onto the airy plateau. What superb views! Keep to the wide cut path and pass through the South entrance of the Roman fort which was built inside the overtaken Iron Age hillfort. Soon you begin to descend to a gap in the rings just like the one where you came in. Go through the gate with the N.T. sign and descend the steep slopes of the field on the other side, with woods on the LH bank leading down to the River Stour, to the exit gate with a Bridleway arrow and follow the track down to the parking area. Now, go down to 'All Together Again'.

THE RIVER STOUR WAY - Walking steadily uphill along the gravel, clay and grass track, there are high hedges on both sides with various gates and openings into the adjacent fields. On the way up, Hod Hill faces you and there are good views back towards Durweston. After a left bend towards the top of the rise and a descent close to the ramparts of Hod Hill on your right, the Bridleway narrows to become a tightly hedged-in gulley with a LH hedge and two large ash trees on the right. *Note: When you get down to the muddy path close to the Stour, you have one last chance to avoid the quagmire by coming back to this spot and taking the unofficial path which winds steeply up through the trees, close to the field fence on the right. At the top of the path, there is a stile in the fence which drops you at the foot of the outer ring. Bear left and follow the outer ring, ascending, until you come to a gate with a N.T. sign. This leads you into a sharply descending field with the steep woods continuing on your left. Pass through the bottom corner gate down to the parking area and go to 'All Together Again'.*

If you stay on the riverside path, go down some root steps and the track becomes narrow, enclosed by trees and full of deep clinging mud. The path continues through trees, honeysuckle and harts tongue fern with the steep slopes of Hod Hill on your right. After a few undulations, the path follows a cut shelf for a while and, although the river remains at the same level below you, you get the distinct impression that you are going uphill. Must be the psychological reaction to all that mud.

However, all trials come to an end and, as the path begins to ascend, it becomes wider and drier for a while with nice views over meadows to the ridge of Okeford Hill beyond on your left. Eventually you reach the dry gravel security of the Hod Hill Car Park..

ALL TOGETHER AGAIN - Go past the Bridleway pointer for 'Stourpaine 1/12' out onto the road - carefully. You can walk along the road to your left all the way to Child Okeford but the road is often quite busy and there is little refuge for the pedestrian for 1.1/2 miles. Far better to come with everybody else and enjoy the fantastic views from the superb ridge walk along Hambledon Hill.

So turn right onto the high-banked road and keep close to the RH side as you ascend between the heavily-wooded slopes of Hod Hill on your right and Hambledon Hill on your left. You will need to cross over to your left before the lay-by near the brow of the hill so that oncoming traffic gets a better view of you - but it's only about 120 yards before you turn off the road again.

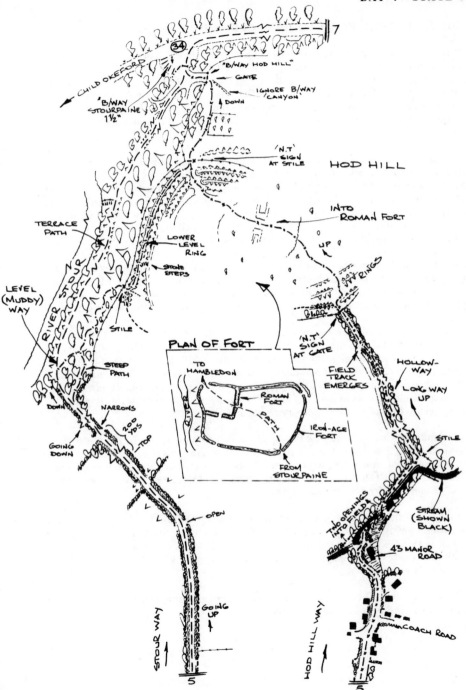

CHILD OKEFORD

"B/WAY
STOURPAINE
1½"

34

"B/WAY HOD HILL"

GATE

IGNORE B/WAY
CANYON

DOWN

'N.T'
SIGN
AT STILE

7

HOD HILL

INTO
ROMAN FORT

TERRACE
PATH

LOWER
LEVEL
RING

UP

RINGS

STONE
STEPS

LEVEL
(MUDDY)
WAY

RIVER STOUR

STILE

'N.T'
SIGN
AT GATE

FIELD
TRACK
EMERGES

HOLLOW-
WAY

LONG WAY
UP

PLAN OF FORT

TO
HAMBLEDON

ROMAN
FORT

RIVER

PATH

IRON-AGE
FORT

FROM
STOUR PAINE

STEEP
PATH

DOWN

NARROWS

200
YDS

TOP

GOING
DOWN

STILE

OPEN

TWO OPENINGS
INTO FIELD

STREAM
(SHOWN
BLACK)

43 MANOR
ROAD

STOUR WAY

GOING
UP

5

HOD HILL WAY

COACH ROAD

5

CHILD OKEFORD ROAD TO HAMBLEDON HILL

At the top of the slope, turn left into the wide concrete junction of tracks and the drive for 'Keepers Cottage'.   Clockwise, the first left track runs into a high field, the second track is the drive into the cottage and the third is yours.   Go through the Bridleway-arrowed farm gate into the high field and turn instantly left to be faced with a very steep chalk track running UP alongside the LH hedge.   Take notice of the 'Dogs worrying livestock will be shot' sign and begin your assault on Hambledon Hill.

Take all the time you need on this breathtaking climb and stop frequently to admire the views unfolding behind you.   If it's any consolation, this is every bit as steep as Scarth Gap Pass in the Lake District - but that has a height increase of about 1500 feet and this has only about 180 feet.   It just feels higher.   Anyway, after the birch, sycamore and ash wood on your left, the track becomes less steep and bends around to the left.   From here, you can see Okeford Hill, Hod Hill and the mast at Blandford Army Camp as you scan the horizon through a red mist from right to left.

Skirting around a Dutch barn, the track passes through a gate with Bridleway arrows. I stopped for a rest here and balanced my cup on the flat top of the LH gatepost. Sadly, the wind blew it off and soaked my back-pack, my camera and my notes with piping hot, much-needed coffee as I was leaning, somewhat heavily, on the gate.

Now, if you've brought a compass with you, it's time for a little practice before you find yourself on the vast open top of Hambledon Hill without any blindingly obvious targets.   Through this gate, the fence runs slightly uphill, beginning at 260 degrees, bearing right to 290, 304 and 326 degrees respectively, following the Southern edge of Coombe Bottom.   All this time, you are following a comfortable grass track, starting with fine views to your left almost to the coast, followed by lovely views to your right to Iwerne Minster, Melbury Down and Shaftesbury.

At a Bridleway-arrowed gate with the top of the ridge up on your left, the fence bears further right to 338 degrees and becomes a levelled grass shelf with a parallel grass track through the descending wood of mostly ash trees cladding the slopes of Coombe Bottom over the RH fence.   The path veers back to 325 degrees - but that's enough. You've undoubtedly got the hang of it now.

At the end of this fence, the grass track bears left and goes, faintly now, over the crest of the hill, passing a stile and a notice inviting foot visitors to explore the open area at will.   Don't go over the stile but go through the Bridleway and Wessex Ridgeway-marked half-gate to its right into a rising, fence-enclosed grass track, still with the woods on your right

All the time, you will be accompanied by the song of skylarks and there is a definite chance of seeing buzzards patrolling the slopes.

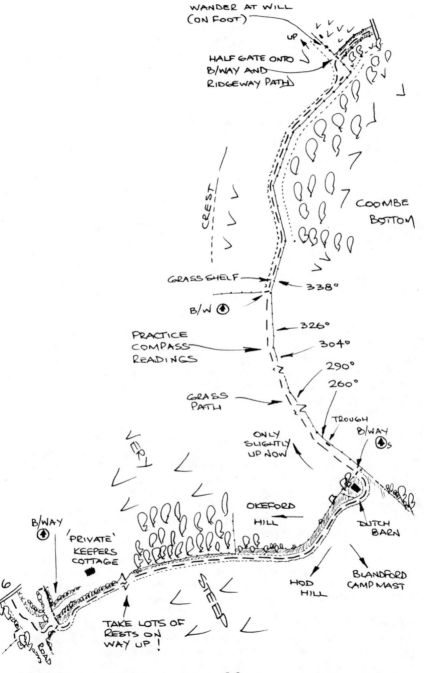

WANDER AT WILL
(ON FOOT)

UP

HALF GATE ONTO
B/WAY AND
RIDGEWAY PATH

CREST

COOMBE
BOTTOM

GRASS SHELF

338°

B/W

326°

PRACTICE
COMPASS
READINGS

304°

290°

260°

GRASS
PATH

TROUGH
B/WAY

ONLY
SLIGHTLY
UP NOW

VERY

OKEFORD
HILL

DUTCH
BARN

B/WAY

'PRIVATE'
KEEPERS
COTTAGE

HOD
HILL

BLANDFORD
CAMP MAST

STEEP

TAKE LOTS OF
RESTS ON
WAY UP!

93

DAY 4 - STAGE 8

HAMBLEDON HILL TO CHILD OKEFORD

The fenced path turns sharp left at another Wessex Ridgeway arrow, leaving the wood's parallel track to continue into an open field.   Ascending (at 320 degrees), the track now widens out as it approaches the Ordnance Survey trig point at 622 feet. The views from here are so extensive, it's hard to believe that you aren't higher than that.   The ramparts of the hill fort look most impressive from this vantage point and there are superb views into the Stour Valley towards Shillingstone and over the Blackmore Vale.

Ignore the right turning Bridleway and W/R arrows and keep straight on, descending towards the half-gate which lets you out of the entrained Bridleway onto the wild, open earthworks of the hilltop settlement.   It is a good mile from here to the North end where you have to descend into the plains of the Stour, so enjoy yourself and spend some time sitting and admiring the landscape below.   Firstly, take out your compass and keep it ready for use.   If you haven't brought one, don't worry.   I'll find some clear reference points to guide you.

Go through the gate and walk straight on, through the first ditch with lovely views over Shroton to the edge of the Cranborne Chase to your right.   Follow the clear path at first until it divides at an arrow indicating where the path for horses follows, more or less, the RH (North-East) slopes of the Hill.   A wide grass track turns left to go up an earthwork alley whilst another, wider, grass track turns right and descends the Hill.   Ignore all of these but bear slightly left, ascending across about 100 yards of open grass to the highest point or peak of Hambledon Hill.

On top of the round peak, those with compasses should take a bearing of 340 degrees and follow it along the top slopes of the Hill before bearing slightly left after 1/2 mile to 320 degrees to the end of the ridge.   Before you set off, a 290 degree WNW bearing will show you Sturminster Newton, the 'capital' of the Blackmore Vale and the end of today's walk, about 3.3/4 miles away as the crow flies.   Everybody else, simply walk along the upper slopes, enjoying the views to both sides but keeping basically to the left of the crest of the Hill and not descending until I tell you.

Right, if you haven't begun a premature descent, you'll suddenly reach the far end of the ridge with a sudden panorama opening out in front.   Another, lower end lies ahead of you (at 320 degrees) straight on.   Walk down to it and look straight ahead. Just below you, there stands a wide, open barn.   To its left, there are greenhouses with a stone house in front of them.   To the left of these, there is a line of trees running from the base of the Hill.   Your path to Child Okeford runs along the right edge of these trees, against the LH edge of the field.   But you can't just walk straight down to this path.   The ramparts are too steep.

Turn left and begin a steady, angular descent until you reach the first path.   Follow it along the side of the Hill (yes, slightly back in the direction you came) until you reach a chalky path which zig-zags steeply down over other paths and over a couple of small ridges towards the clear, bald convergence of paths at the bottom gate.

A 'Hambledon Hill' board lurks behind a bush near the kissing gate (with a painted yellow arrow on a post).   Go through the gate onto a root-stepped path which descends between the aforementioned row of trees and the field fence on your right.

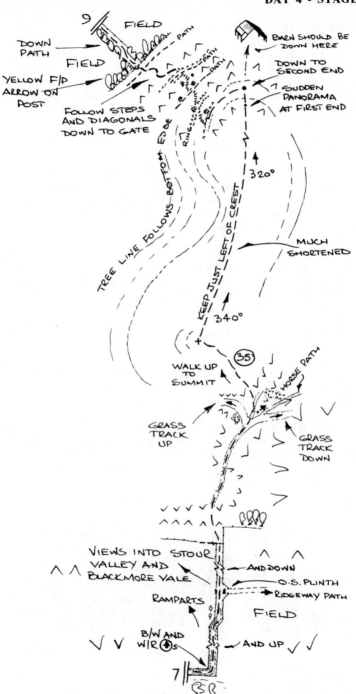

DAY 4 - STAGE 9

THROUGH CHILD OKEFORD

Keep on down the ash and sycamore-lined path to the stile at the bottom.   Go over the stile and walk down to join the road, turning left opposite Hambledon Cottage. After Hambledon View and the Child Okeford Surgery on the right, the pointed windows of the thatched Gothic Cottage on the left are interesting.   At the end of the lane (Upper Street), you emerge at a junction with the Manston/Gillingham road but you won't be anywhere near there until Day 5.   Follow the LH hedge around the corner to visit St Nicholas' church, Child Okeford.   Largely rebuilt, the 15thC tower remains and there is a 1568 bible in a glass case inside.

Hutchins suggests that the name of the village stems from its "chill" situation but, as it lies in the shelter of Hambledon Hill, this may be something of a flight of fancy. The Okeford part refers to "ancient oaks which stood in or near the ford" - this is more likely.   Listed in the Domesday Book as 'Acford', the king's land under the ownership of the Count of Mortain, it once boasted two mills on the Stour.

Back outside, the War Memorial cross is situated on the little island opposite Cross Cottage and the Baker Arms.   After a rest on the steps, continue along High Street through the village but only as far as the first turning on the right, Haywards Lane - a hayward being the gentleman in charge of keeping lost or strayed livestock in the village pound until the owner claimed them and paid for their keep whilst in 'storage'.

Down this lane, go past a superb twin-gabled house with a leaded porch and a covering of laburnum - a high, sloping brick wall supporting its garden.   At the cross-lanes with Jacob's Ladder on the left and Rectory Lane on the right, keep straight on down the lane with high hedges on either side.   At the next junction, with Jacob's Ladder again on the left, turn sharp right onto a gravel track - before the Greenway estate also on the right.

Follow the RH hedge around the returning bend and you'll find a Footpath sign for 'Haywards Bridge 1' pointing over a stile next to a gate in the LH hedge.   The track keeps straight on but go over the stile instead.   You will find yourself in a 30 yards wide, fenced grassy track with high trees on the left and about 20 new, framed trees lining the RH fence.   Begin a nice, level walk along this grassy lane/narrow field.

Looking back up the path from Hambledon Hill

9 6

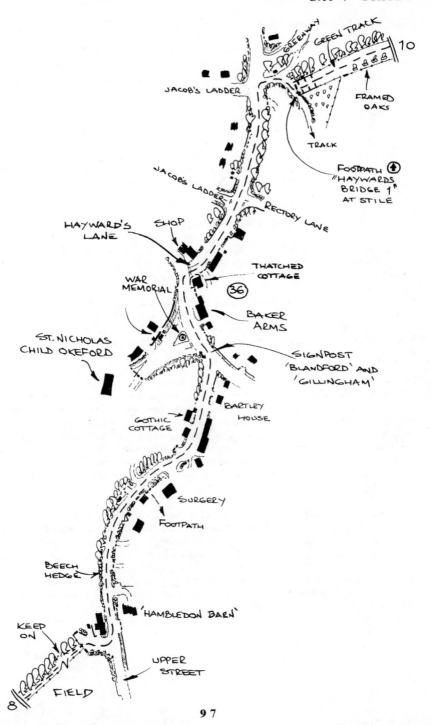

10

GREENWAY   GREEN TRACK

FRAMED
OAKS

JACOB'S LADDER

TRACK

FOOTPATH ⊕
"HAYWARDS
BRIDGE 1"
AT STILE

JACOB'S LADDER

RECTORY LANE

HAYWARD'S
LANE   SHOP

THATCHED
COTTAGE

WAR
MEMORIAL   (36)

BAKER
ARMS

ST. NICHOLAS
CHILD OKEFORD

SIGNPOST
'BLANDFORD' AND
'GILLINGHAM'

GOTHIC
COTTAGE   BARTLEY
HOUSE

SURGERY

FOOTPATH

BEECH
HEDGE

'HAMBLEDON BARN'

KEEP
ON

UPPER
STREET

8   FIELD

9 7

DAY 4 - STAGE 10

CHILD OKEFORD TO NEWMANS DROVE

Leaving the wide 'alley' at a stile in the RH end, bear half-right in the next level field and aim for the gate and stile in the far RH corner. The stile rails are very highly polished due to popular usage but there aren't any Footpath arrows. Hopefully, there will be some along here soon. I *have* asked for some.

Over this stile, the next field is L-shaped (in reverse) and the exit is about 1/4 mile away at the narrower end, 3/4 of the way from the LH hedge and 1/4 of the way from the RH hedge. Arriving at the stile and gate, the path goes straight on towards a single sleeper across a drainage ditch (276 degrees WNW if you're still using your compass). But, if the ground is dry and the grass not too long, you can head directly at 230 degrees from this stile towards the River Stour bridge without going over the little footbridge at all.

But, from the sleeper bridge, bear left and aim for the wooden rails of the River Stour footbridge which you will be able to make out about 300 yards away. Now, however you arrived at the concrete-decked bridge across the River Stour, you will find willows on both, steep-sided banks and reeds in the bed on your right. Cross the stiles at either end and stop to watch the river for a few minutes.

On the other side, bear half-right again (210 degrees) and follow the long, well-walked path across open meadowland past two willows on the right and two smaller trees on the left. This leads to another steel-rail and concrete footbridge over the meandering Stour. Cross over this bridge and bear very slightly right again, not far from the RH fence with trees behind it.

Passing one side or the other of a single hawthorn bush, cross this end of the open field, aiming for the left end of the bungalow across the tarmac drive. There may not be official Footpath arrows yet, but this is the true direction. (However, be prepared to follow the RH fence as it zig-zags anti-clockwise around this end of the field. You actually want to get to the gate and cattle-grid which straddle the tarmac track at the other end of the bungalow). On reaching the bungalow and the tarmac lane at 'Newmans Drove', turn right and walk up to the gate and cattle grid. Cross over the grid onto the tarmac drive with a track running off into 'Bere Marsh Farm' farmyard on your left.

Keep straight on along the drive (or drove) and go through the facing gate onto a long, straight tarmac track with a wire-fenced field on the left. Incidentally, the gate next to an old brick barn on your right, before this drive gate, is the exit from another unsigned Footpath and there is a slight possibility that it may have been re-instated by now. Anyway, with cattle sorting pens in the LH field and a wide, open grassy area on your right, keep straight on to another gate in a wooden fence across your track. Go through this gate as well and follow the left-bending track past another old, low brick barn on your right.

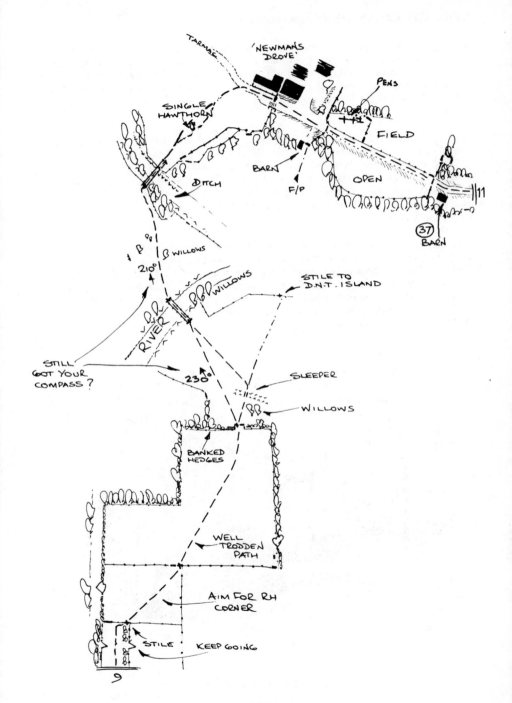

DAY 4 - STAGE 11

NEWMANS DROVE TO STOUR FIELDS

Along the track, you pass a Bridleway path running into a deep, narrow wood on the left and, shortly after that, the field narrows into a verged driveway with a much-restored and extended cottage on the left. Go through the Bridleway-arrowed gate across your path where the track runs out and into the wide, grassy area on the other side. Take note of the first of many 'Please Keep the Get Shut' signs (PKTGS from now on).

Here, on the uphill slope, there is a track going down on your reverse right and a wire-fenced vineyard up the slope to your left. Keep to the right of the vineyard and, past this, the winding track becomes clear with a deep slope on the right followed by hedges to right and left. Go through the next PKTGS gate and follow the undulations of the next field, past 'Diggers Copse' on your right, until you reach a stile and farm gate on your right. Keep straight on up the field, keeping close to 'Ham Down Copse' on your right.

Arriving at another Bridleway-arrowed PKTGS gate in the hedge in the top RH corner, go through and walk 150 yards straight across the open field (324 degrees) aiming for the LH end of the opposite hedge and trees. You want a spot 2/3 of the way from the LH electricity post and 1/3 from the RH electricity post. Then follow the fenced edge of the RH wood to the next Bridleway and PKTGS-signed gate. Now keep near to the hedge and the new strip of ash and willows on your left through this next, slightly rising - and much wider - field.

Hammoon Manor House - on Stage 12

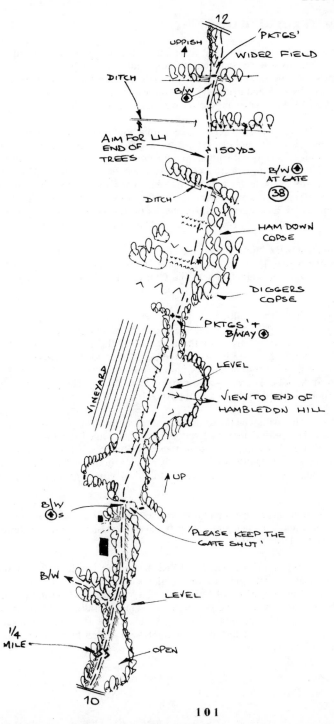

12

UPPISH

'PKTGS'
WIDER FIELD

DITCH

B/W

AIM FOR LH
END OF
TREES

150YDS

B/W
AT GATE

38

DITCH

HAM DOWN
COPSE

DIGGERS
COPSE

'PKTGS' +
B/WAY

LEVEL

VINEYARD

VIEW TO END OF
HAMBLEDON HILL

UP

B/W
S

'PLEASE KEEP THE
GATE SHUT'

B/W

LEVEL

1/4
MILE

OPEN

10

101

STOUR FIELDS THROUGH HAMMOON

Keeping to the grass track, follow this 300 yards long field, levelling out now, to the next PKTGS and Bridleway-arrowed gate into the next field.   Through this gate, keep to the winding grass track near to the hedge on your left with the long, lower field on your right.   One more PKTGS and Bridleway-arrowed gate brings you into a 450 yards long level field where the track becomes clearer with grass up the middle.

Finally, you emerge through the last PKTGS gate, with a wire fence on its right and a hedge on its left, onto a gravel and chalk farm track which the hedge continues to accompany, past a brick cottage and garden on the right, to its end.   Turn left at the junction with the tarmac road a few yards ahead where a concrete track runs off on the RH corner to some barns.   The hedge runs down to a series of farm gates on your left with an assortment of barns beyond them.   On the opposite side, a stone wall protects the perimeter of East Farm and, on the wood-fenced corner, a signpost confirms that you have come on the Bridleway from 'Haywards Bridge 1.3/4'.

At the road junction where the stone garden wall of 'Hammoon House' on your right ends at a postbox, the road to the right goes to Manston and Child Okeford whilst the road opposite leads to a convenient bench, the Church of St Paul and Hammoon Manor House.

Hammoon derives its name from William de Moion who "brought 47 knights to the Battle of Hastings" in 1066.   St Paul's Church escaped the rebuilding excesses of the Victorian era and was simply enhanced by the addition of the bell turret in 1885, The nave and chancel are 12th and 13thC whilst the pulpit was added in 1635.   The smart 15thC reredos is not original to this church but was brought here from a stonemasons' yard in London where it was discovered in 1945.   The stone carving depicts the Crucifixion flanked by figures of the Apostles.

The Manor House is roofed with reed thatch and has stone-mullioned, arched windows of the Tudor period.   The unique porch, a later addition, has ringed baroque columns on either side of the arched opening similar to those on Ruben's house in Antwerp. Now, press on down the road, parallel to the one on which you arrived in Hammoon, past the telephone box on your right and with houses on your right and 'Victory Cottages' on your left.

After about 1/2 mile, past several gates and high-banked hedges on both sides of the road and after the 'Hammoon' nameplate, you arrive at a gravel and chalk Bridleway which turns off right to 'Fiddleford 1.1/4'.

Turn onto this track between a LH wire fence and a RH hedge and you'll see the Rixon end of Sturminster Newton straight ahead.   The stone church and prominent buildings up on the distant hill, North of Sturminster Newton, are at Hinton St Mary and the houses about 1 mile away on the slopes to the right of Hinton St Mary are at the village of Manston.   Go through the gate which crosses the track and keep following the track as it turns first left and then right with a high hedge on the left and a wire fenced field on the right.

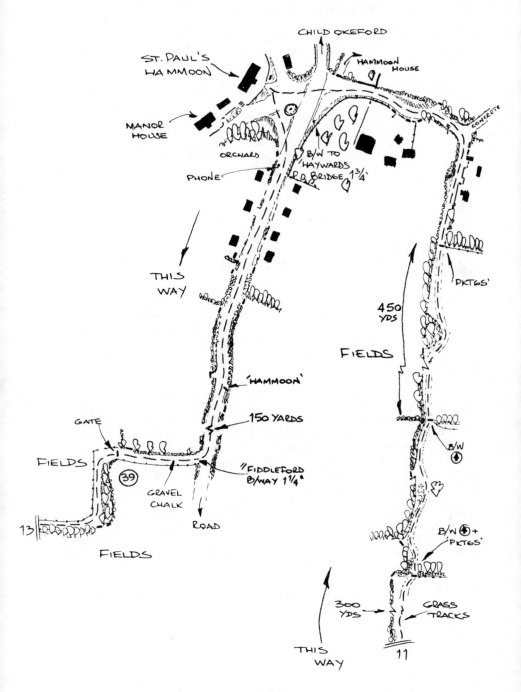

CHILD OKEFORD

ST. PAUL'S HAMMOON

HAMMOON HOUSE

MANOR HOUSE

ORCHARD

PHONE

B/W TO HAYWARDS R.B. BRIDGE 1¾'

CONCRETE

THIS WAY

PKT 6S'

450 YDS

FIELDS

'HAMMOON'

150 YARDS

GATE

FIELDS

39

GRAVEL CHALK

"FIDDLEFORD B/WAY 1¼'

ROAD

13

FIELDS

B/W

B/W + PKT 6S'

300 YDS

GRASS TRACKS

11

THIS WAY

HAMMOON TO FIDDLEFORD MILL

Keep following the track as it bends slightly right and a farm gate appears in the hedge on your left. A Bridleway pointer directs you through this gate whilst there is a barn further along the track you are leaving.

Go left through the gate into a 1/4 mile long field with a fence, a hedge and some trees on your left. Aim for a spot in the hedge on the far side of the field about 20 yards from the far LH corner. On the way across, you cannot fail to notice what appears to be a ridge and furrow field system spread across the field on your right, running parallel to your path. I'm sure the historians amongst you will know exactly what it is. Anyway, nearing the far side, you will see a half-gate in the hedge. Head straight for it, go through and cross the wooden bridge over a small stream in a strip of trees into a narrow field, tapering into a new wood on your left.

Follow the path, at a slight angle to the right, across the corner of this field to a gate in the hedge opposite. The railway track from Stourpaine and Durweston Halt to Sturminster Newton used to run on the track behind this gate. Go up the embankment to a Bridleway pointer and turn right to follow the grass, clinker and gravel line between low fields for about 100 yards. There are good views to Hinton St Mary over on the front right.

When the track emerges from being hedged-in on both sides by elderberries, hawthorns, beech and oak, it continues straight on with openings into all of the fields at this junction. Keep following the old track, ignoring the grass track which turns off into the LH field, until you arrive at the next junction of tracks and corner entrances into various fields with a twin-pointer of Bridleway arrows on the near LH corner.

Here, the extension of the old line is less clear and has a line of electricity poles running alongside it. Don't follow it! It isn't the Bridleway and it only leads to a sudden drop into the River Stour where there used to be a railway bridge. Anyway, it's private. Instead, turn left onto the track which runs between hedges for about 250 yards. On the way to join a tarmac lane at a T-junction, the track passes a high yard of barns behind the LH hedge. At the junction, with a sign for 'Hammoon 1' facing you, turn right onto the level lane with a verge, ditch and hedge on the right and a verge, stream and woods on the left.

In about 100 yards, the stream runs under the road, prefaced by a Footpath-arrowed stile in the RH hedge. The lane turns left, signed for 'Fiddleford Manor and Car Park', but keep straight on towards the group of buildings ahead, signed for 'Sturminster Newton 1' and 'Fiddleford Mill House B and B' - seems like a very good idea to me.

Follow the verged drive to the wide entrance gate, with a Footpath arrow on the half-gate alongside, and into the yard of Fiddleford Mill.

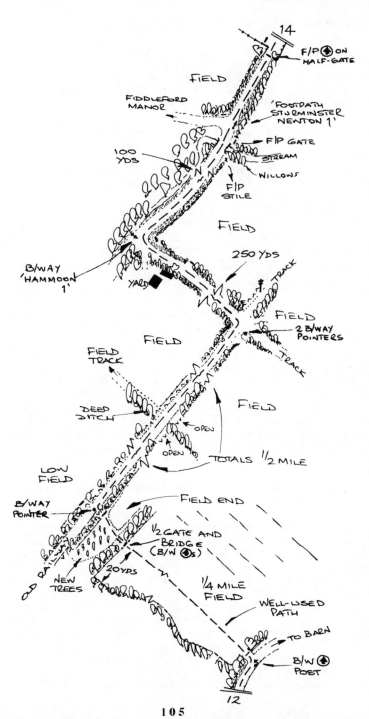

14

F/P ● ON
HALF-GATE

FIELD

FIDDLEFORD
MANOR

'FOOTPATH
STURMINSTER
NEWTON 1'

F/P GATE

100
YDS

STREAM

WILLOWS

F/P
STILE

FIELD

250 YDS

B/WAY
'HAMMOON
1'

YARD

TRACK

FIELD

2 B/WAY
POINTERS

FIELD

TRACK

FIELD
TRACK

FIELD

DEEP
DITCH

OPEN

OPEN

TOTALS ½ MILE

LOW
FIELD

B/WAY
POINTER

FIELD END

½ GATE AND
BRIDGE
(B/W ●s)

OLD RAILWAY

20 YDS

¼ MILE
FIELD

NEW
TREES

WELL-USED
PATH

TO BARN

B/W ●
POST

12

105

DAY 4 - STAGE 14

FIDDLEFORD MILL TO PENNY STREET

Keep straight on through the Mill yard, passing buildings to right and left. As you go under the roof between the mill itself and the attached house, note the medieval plaque on the RH wall. Follow the fenced path round to the left, past the headwaters on your left and the turbulent waters below the sluice on your right. There is a lovely view back to the mullioned stone Manor house and garden over the river from here. Following the concrete path across the small, wooded island, cross the weir bridge and emerge into the field on the other side through a kissing-gate with two Footpath arrows. The sign beyond offers two ways to Sturminster Newton - the Railway Path to the right at 1.1/4 miles and the direct route straight on at 1 mile. The Railway Path leads uninterestingly along the track to the town car park but the direct route takes you into the centre of the town. This is the one you need.

Anyway, go through the kissing gate, cross the short field to the hedge facing you and go over the narrow, stiled and arrowed concrete bridge over a tree-lined ditch into the long field which runs between the river on your left and a banked hedge over on your right. The path is now a wide grass path cut through the meadow (generally at 276 degrees) and it aims straight for the gap in the distant hedge, against the RH higher hedge. It's about 550 yards to the gap into the next field and, just before you reach it, a gate in the RH hedge leads onto a wide, grass track lined with old oak trees.

Arriving at the gap with a Footpath arrow, just keep close to the RH hedge now, bending right after a vast oak tree to a stile and a gate with another Footpath arrow.

Go over the stile into the field and turn half-left (310 degrees) and stop. Look ahead to select a couple of electricity poles - the LH one having house roofs behind it and the RH one having open sky behind it. Got them? St Mary's church will be ahead, a little to your left, if you're in the right direction. Aim at the LH pole and pass just to its left when you get nearer. On reaching a collection of gates and stiles, with a grass track coming between the fence and hedge on your right hand, select the stile which leads onto an enclosed path between a rough yard and a high hedge. It is signposted for 'Penny Street 1/4' whilst the stile into the field *which you don't want* is arrowed and signed for 'Railway Path 1/4'.

Climb over the stile and head up the narrow path between the wire-fenced yard and the LH row of trees and bushes.

When you reach the end of this path, a right turn into Penny Street will take you directly up into Sturminster Newton and the route is described in Stage 15. If you decide to go that way, rather than the path through the churchyard which is also shown on the Stage 15 map, don't look into anybody's windows until you have passed Gotts Corner. I have had all the collective sins of the country's ramblers laid firmly at my door by a lady who lives here because walkers who pass her cottage to and from the Public Footpaths in the area appear unable to resist looking in. Clearly, it is all my fault. She told me she has had to have blinds fitted and that I should "Go back where I came from". Anyway, to cut a long story short, I promised to tell you to take the St Mary's route - although this means you won't see the house where William Barnes was given his first job. However, if you do take the Penny Street option, you must all promise to behave yourselves. Then, I may be forgiven in the fulness of time (apart from coming from the Midlands, that is). Who knows?

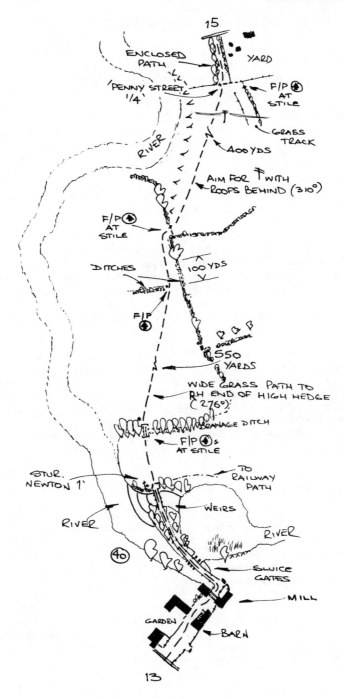

15

ENCLOSED PATH

YARD

PENNY STREET 1/4'

F/P ⊕ AT STILE

GRASS TRACK

RIVER

400 YDS

AIM FOR ✝ WITH ROOFS BEHIND (310°)

F/P ⊕ AT STILE

DITCHES

100 YDS

F/P ⊕

550 YARDS

WIDE GRASS PATH TO RH END OF HIGH HEDGE (270°)

DRAINAGE DITCH

F/P ⊕s AT STILE

STUR. NEWTON 1'

TO RAILWAY PATH

WEIRS

RIVER

RIVER

40

SLUICE GATES

MILL

GARDEN

BARN

13

107

PENNY STREET TO STURMINSTER NEWTON

Now is the time to decide whether you want to visit St Mary's and enjoy the view from the churchyard over the Stour or to walk directly up into the town past Thomas Dashwood's house where young William Barnes was given his first job - at the age of thirteen.

FOR THE CHURCH: Turn left into Penny's Lane and follow it round to the steps up into the churchyard of St Mary's with a huge Douglas fir tree on your right and the views over the Stour on your left.   This is a much larger church than others you have visited already and, although it was largely rebuilt in 1827, it managed to keep its 15thC nave and its North and South aisles.   The 15thC tower was much restored whilst the old wagon roof of the nave is of special interest.   After your visit, leave the churchyard ahead of the doors and follow Church Street round to join Penny's Lane again on its exit into Sturminster Newton Market Square.

FOR MR DASHWOOD'S: Turn right up Penny Street and begin to walk uphill towards the town - carefully avoiding looking at the row of cottages on your right before Gotts Corner..   I noticed some time ago that there are a number of streets on the edges of some towns and country villages with old coinage in their names and I was recently told by a countryman that these recall the days when sheep or cattle which were on the move to or from market or farms were 'parked' overnight in rented fields for which the charge was in the region of a 'Farthing', a 'Halfpenny' or a 'Penny'.

Continue up the road to the long, stone mullion-windowed Vine House.   This is where the boy William Barnes, the greatest ever Dorset dialect poet, was given his first job as a clerk for Thomas Dashwood, the solicitor.   Whilst William Barnes' poetic works are known nationally, it is less well-known that, besides Latin and Greek, he counted a knowledge of seventeen other languages amongst his academic achievements.   The Lane Fox Terrace row of cottages up on your left was once the old Endowed School where Barnes was educated until 1814 when he left to join Mr Dashwood at the age of thirteen - having been chosen for his excellent handwriting.

Now, past the turning which gives a second opportunity to visit St Mary's, keep straight on to the top of Penny's Lane and then bear right into Market Square.

EVERYBODY: The constituent parts of the town's name are almost self-explanatory.   On this North side of the medieval ten-arched bridge, which was widened in the 17thC and lengthened over the adjoining wetland in 1825, stands *Sturminster* named from 'Stour', the river and 'Minster', the church.   On the South side stands the separate hamlet of *Newton* or "New Town".   Little now remains of Newton Castle except the mound on which it stood - on the other side of the main road beyond the bridge.

The ancient market, only recently disbanded after 600 years, was held on Mondays further on in Station Road.   However, whilst you are here, you cannot help but notice that Sturminster Newton (or just "Stur" to the locals) is crammed with pubs, restaurants and hotels - just the place to end the Day.

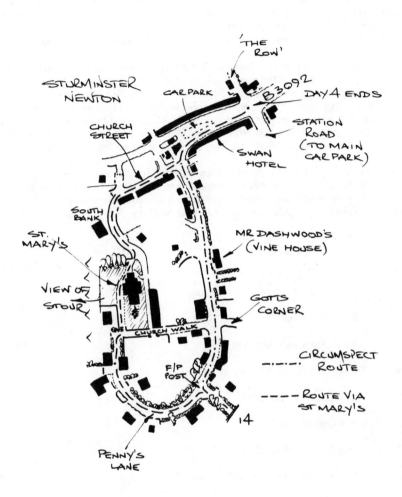

'THE ROW'

STURMINSTER NEWTON

CAR PARK

B 3092

DAY 4 ENDS

STATION ROAD (TO MAIN CAR PARK)

CHURCH STREET

SWAN HOTEL

SOUTH BANK

ST. MARY'S

MR DASHWOOD'S (VINE HOUSE)

VIEW OF STOUR

GOTTS CORNER

ONE

CHURCH WALK

CIRCUMSPECT ROUTE

F/P POST

ROUTE VIA ST MARY'S

14

PENNY'S LANE

DAY 5 - INTRODUCTION

STURMINSTER NEWTON TO WYKE CROSSROADS

This is a completely different Day - no more hill forts to climb. You're on altogether easier country now as the River Stour meanders from one pretty Dorset village to another throughout the whole of Day 5. You cross the river on several occasions and walk right by its edge many times. Whereas you were forced to lose contact with the river quite a few times on Day 4, this stage seldom wanders very far away. You'll keep coming across it (much younger than it was) at unexpected moments.

The Day begins in the market town of Sturminster Newton and immediately offers a long stroll by the edge of the river as an alternative to visiting the lovely village of Hinton St Mary. During the Day, you can visit four fine inns and, balancing the secular, you can also visit four really lovely churches. There are a few strange tales along the way and you go past more watermills, all powered by our river. All in all, this is quite an easy Day filled with delightful villages, meadows and gently sloping fields. There is much variety and there are many pastoral delights in store.

Before you go - The New Stour Valley Path no longer offers a direct route from Fifehead Magdalen to West Stour. It used to mean a 200 yards dash along the A30 at the far end and I was never really happy about it - and now that this Day is shorter than it was in the 1st edition, a chance to visit Stour Provost is far too good to miss.

	STAGE	MILES	TOTAL MILES
1	Sturminster Newton to River Stour	.50	41.50
2	River Stour and Twinwood Coppice	.50	42
3	River Stour and Hinton St Mary	.50	42.50
4	Stour and Hinton St Mary to Yardgrove	.75	43.25
5	Yardgrove to Marnhull	1	44.25
6	Through Marnhull	.75	45
7	Marnhull to Fifehead Magdalen	1.25	46.25
8	Fifehead Magdalen to Stour Provost	1	47.25
9	Stour Provost to West Stour	1	48.25
10	West Stour to Stour Fields	1	49.25
11	Stour Fields to Nations Road	.75	50
12	Nations Road to Thorngrove Lodge	.75	50.75
13	Thorngrove Lodge to Wyke Crossroads	.75	51.50

STURMINSTER NEWTON TO WYKE CROSSROADS

Church of St Mary Magdalene, Fifehead Magdalen

Cutt Mill near Hinton St Mary (from Bagber path)

DAY 5 - STAGE 1

STURMINSTER NEWTON TO RIVER STOUR

Having explored Sturminster Newton, leave by the B3092 and turn left into the narrow 'The Row' opposite Station Road . Passing the Old Chapel on your left, you emerge onto the wider road coming past Sturminster Hall on the right. Keep straight on between houses and cottages and Bonslea Mead.

The lane ends at a kissing gate between the RH garden hedge and a LH fence and the path into the end field is signposted 'Road Lane Farm 1.1/2 and Colber Bridge 1/4'.. Follow the gradient of the grassy slope, past a Footpath arrow post and close to the LH fence and hedge, down to a stile and gate in the hedge at the bottom. There is another stile in the LH hedge but go over the one facing you.

Over the stile, a Footpath signpost points back up to 'Market Place 1/4' and to 'Hinton St Mary 1.1/2' to your right. Other paths go to Sturminster Newton Mill and Stalbridge Lane but you have to turn right for Hinton St Mary. So, turn off the path which goes to the white-painted, iron Colber Bridge and walk parallel to the river on your left with new trees and a high hedge on your right. This area is frequently quite wet underfoot so tread circumspectly.

As the high hedge and embankment trees come nearer, go under the arch of the partially demolished railway bridge which no longer spans the river - although its approach sections are still intact on both sides. There is still a painted yellow arrow on the brickwork between the two arches. On the other side, follow the meandering path through a new plantation of small trees with marshy ground all around you.

Colber Bridge from Stalbridge Lane side

112

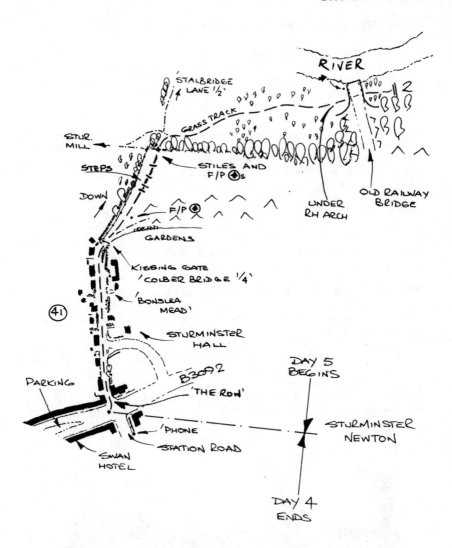

RIVER

'STALBRIDGE
LANE ½'

GRASS TRACK

STUR.
MILL

STEPS

STILES AND
F/P ⊕s

DOWN

F/P ⊕

GARDENS

UNDER
RH ARCH

OLD RAILWAY
BRIDGE

KISSING GATE
'COLBER BRIDGE ¼'

'BONSLEA
MEAD'

(41)

STURMINSTER
HALL

B3092

DAY 5
BEGINS

PARKING

'THE ROW'

STURMINSTER
NEWTON

'PHONE

STATION ROAD

SWAN
HOTEL

DAY 4
ENDS

RIVER STOUR AND TWINWOOD COPPICE

Between the river and the embankment, squelch your way through the new trees and over the wooden sleepers to a slight river terrace and up to an old tree stump.   Go over the Footpath-arrowed stile just past this stump in the RH corner and follow the uphill, Footpath-signed, path to the top of the slope where a stile and a Footpath-signed gate leads onto a hedged track up to the B3092.

However, keep on your original path and head down towards a cattle trough.   Now, you have to decide whether to follow the river for a pleasant 1.1/2 miles and join the others at Cutt Mill or go and visit the church, stone tithe barn and village of Hinton St Mary instead.   Whichever you decide, you'll be missing a treat so you'd better come back another day to enjoy the other option.

RIVERSIDE WALK: Don't pass the cattle trough!   Bear left towards the river and cross the Footpath and Hardy Way-signed footbridge over the ditch which runs into the Stour.   Follow the river's edge to go over a set of two arrowed stiles and three bridges through the narrow end of Twinwood Coppice.   No more instructions for now.   Just enjoy the River.

FOR HINTON ST MARY: Pass the trough and keep on the higher path, bearing away from the River and parallel to the slope from the right, until you arrive at a stile in the wire fence across your route. Go over the Footpath-arrowed stile and over a handrailed footbridge which crosses a wide ditch, into a mixed beech, hazel, sycamore and oak wood.   This is Twinwood Coppice and a sign just off the path to your right soon reminds you that these are 'Private Woods. Keep Out'.   Go past the Footpath arrow post on the other side and up the bank into an uphill field .   A cut grass path around the meandering edge of the field follows the ditch and edge of Twinwood Coppice.   In about 400 yards, the path takes a left bend where a sign beyond the ditch advises 'Keep Out. Police Parkwatch'.   Just keep on going up and around this long field edge.

Manor House, Hinton St Mary - On Stage 3

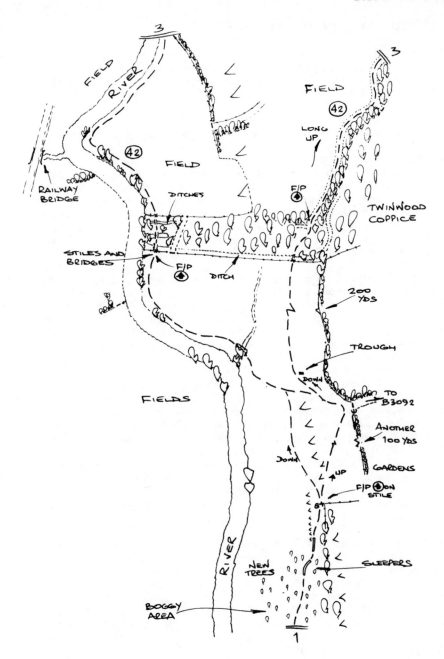

DAY 5 - STAGE 3

RIVER STOUR AND HINTON ST MARY

RIVERSIDE WALK: Just keep enjoying the level stroll along the river's edge, passing through two Footpath-arrowed bridge and stile complexes on the way. After the last stile on your map, if you line up the riverside tree with the oak in the field, you'll see Cutt Mill in the distance. This is where you meet the Hinton St Mary visitors again.

HINTON ST MARY: Eventually, the grass track bears right as the field tapers to a point in the top RH corner. Go past the pair of big oaks in the LH hedge, past the right-turn to the high 'Private. Keep out' gates and the opening into the RH field to join a hedged track. Follow the short track to a gate across your route at the end. You emerge onto a slightly rising tarmac lane with a Footpath signpost pointing back to 'Sturminster Newton 1.14'. Turn right onto the road with verges, ditches and hedges on either side. Keep straight on, past farm gates in both sides and, after a couple of bungalows and cottages, carefully cross the B3092 which you left behind at Sturminster Newton. On the opposite corner, there is a 'phone box, then a raised stone pavement on the LH side. Follow the uphill lane into Hinton St Mary.

The village derives the first part of its name from a Saxon owner whilst the second part comes from the Abbey of St Mary in Shaftesbury which is recorded in the Domesday Book as holding *Haintone*. St Peter's church still has its 12thC font and a 15thC Perpendicular tower although it was extensively rebuilt by William Osborne in 1846. On your arrival at the top of the hill, go and have a look at the church which stands in the RH lane over on the left - and the Manor House next door. This was built in 1695 and is owned by the Pitt-Rivers family. It was once home to the famous archaeologist George Pitt-Rivers but, long before him, it was owned by the mystical writer William Freke who specialised in the interpretation of dreams and produced a Dictionary of Dreams. Between 1683 and 1687, Freke fell foul of the legal and religious Establishments by publishing an eight-part essay which included "a clear and brief confutation of the Doctrine of the Divinity". He sent the essays to Members of Parliament who voted them to be burnt in the Palace Yard. Freke was bound over for 3 years and ordered to make recantation in the four Courts of Westminster Hall. Later, after his arrival here, he came to believe that he was a prophet but, despite this, he became a Justice of the Peace for Hinton St Mary. He died in 1744 at the age of 82 and was buried in the churchyard next door. After your visit, or instead if you prefer, you can rest awhile on the bench opposite the 'White Horse' but don't forget you've a long way to go yet.

Go back the way you came to the B3092 and cross over to the pavement by the Bus Shelter. Walk on along the pavement until you reach a garage/workshop on your left. Turn left onto the drive which leads to the yard behind the garage. Bearing right across the concrete yard, you will find a Footpath-arrowed gate between a shed and a barn directly beyond the thatched house's garden. On the other side of the gate, follow a line at 280 degrees WNW. Or turn half left, away from the RH hedge with the willows in it, and aim for the single small tree 200 yards away in the LH hedge. On the way diagonally across this field, you will see a stile in the hedge. Go straight to it and you'll find a Footpath arrow. Go over the stile, into the ditch and over the bank (all in the wide hedge) to the stile on the other side. Stop again and turn half-right (280 degrees still), aiming for the stile and gate which isn't very far down the wire fence on your right.

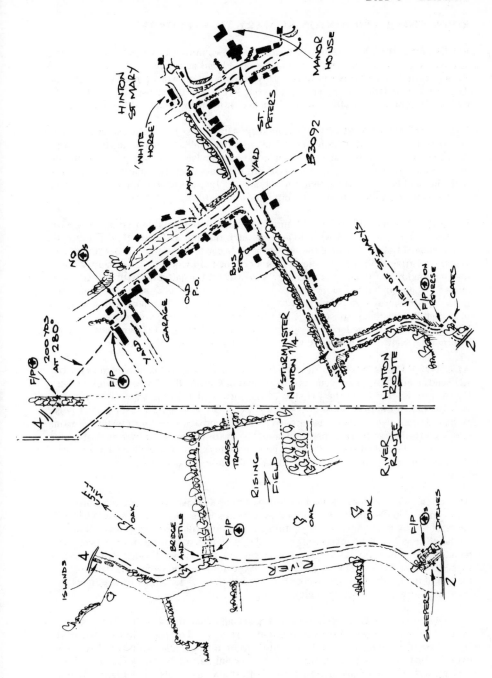

DAY 5 - STAGE 4

RIVER STOUR AND HINTON ST MARY TO YARDGROVE

RIVERSIDE WALK: Follow the edge, past a few immature islands, to a Footpath-arrowed stile which leads into a plantation of old and new trees. Follow the oft-arrowed path through the newer trees until you reach a narrowing, fenced area between the RH woods and the cottage garden on your left. Up the steps, go over the stile with the 'Sturminster Newton 2 miles' sign and turn left for your visit to Cutt Mill.

FROM HINTON ST MARY: Cutting diagonally across this field corner, go over the Footpath-arrowed stile in the fence and cross over the 20 yards wide strip field to the wide cut edge on the far side, against the high hedge. Don't go through the opening into the next field but turn left, down the grass track as it goes over the brow of the hill and heads down the field for 1/4 mile. Just enjoy the views unfolding in front of you - but don't fall over any big weeds in the track.

Before the bottom of this strip field, turn right through the wood-fenced opening with Bridleway and Footpath arrows onto a grass track through a sloping field filled with newly-planted trees. Do what the notice says - 'Keep to the Path'. After about 150 yards, you arrive in the far, bottom LH corner of the field/wood. Turn sharply down into the muddy dip in this corner where you will find a half-gate with a Bridleway arrow. Go through into a narrow strip of wood and out the other side onto Cutt Mill Lane. A Bridleway sign points back to 'Wood Lane 3/4'. The route continues up to your right but you really must visit Cutt Mill on the Stour before you go on. So turn left and go down the hedged lane, past a stile and a sign on a LH bend pointing to 'Sturminster Newton 2' where the Riverside walkers join the rest of you.

ALL TOGETHER AGAIN: Keep on down the lane, past a bank of new trees on the RH bend and the cottage on your left, to its end at Cutt Mill. A footbridge crosses the river to 'Bagber 1' on the LH side of the Mill whilst, to the right of it, you can walk out onto a walkway above two sluice gates. The wonderful Dorset dialect poet, William Barnes, who I briefly mentioned on your approach into Sturminster Newton, was born in Bagber in 1801 and he learned to swim in the Stour by a bed of water lilies (clotes, he calls them). It would be nice to think that it could have been near to this spot. There are dozens of water lilies in the calm waters above the sluice gates in summer.

After a brief visit, go back up the lane and past the gate where you came out onto Cutt Mill Lane. Up the lane a little further, go past opposing barriers and, in another 100 yards, at an oak tree in the LH hedge, turn left at a Footpath post and go over the stile on the other side of the banked hedge. In the field, turn right for just a few paces and then follow the high-up RH hedge. On a clear day, you can see Pilsdon Pen, Dorset's highest peak at 911ft, at 240 degrees South West from the gap in the RH hedge. At the end of the hedge, turn right a couple of yards before the far corner by a post with a Footpath arrow (at the wrong angle).

Up in this next field, keep close to the LH hedge and then, in about 30 yards, go over the twin stiles either side of the beech hedge. There is a Footpath arrow on the other side. Now, keep to the RH wire fence - high up on a wide ridge with excellent views over the lush dairy and arable fields of this special part of North Dorset and to the ever-present, wooded Duncliffe Hill, to Shaftesbury up on its high plateau and to Melbury Downs over on your right.

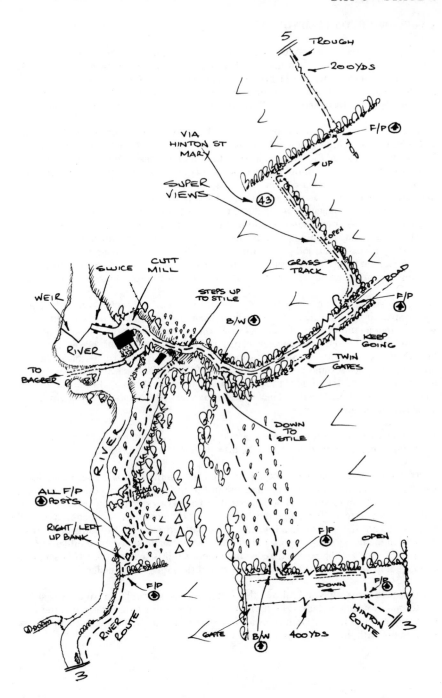

DAY 5 - STAGE 5

YARDGROVE TO MARNHULL

There is sometimes a temporary electric fence across this field in about 200 yards time. I haven't drawn it on the map because it wasn't there on my final check. Whatever, keep to the RH wire fence, past a cattle trough and straight on to a stile in the top RH corner - without any arrows on your side. If you're coming the other way, you have both Footpath and Hardy Way arrows. Life can be so unfair sometimes.

Go over the stile and follow the path between the RH wire fence and some LH willows and elderberries, behind which lurks a small pool. In a few yards, you are confronted by two stiles. Ignore the one which goes straight on but take the RH one. This has two Footpath arrows. Follow the line of the hedge on your right aiming generally for the red-tiled roof ahead of you. Again, this grassy, anti-clockwise edge to the field may or may not be electric-fenced in. I've drawn it in this time because it seems to be becoming permanent. If it's there, the lift-off part is just by the LH corner, so you don't have to crawl under or climb over it. Then, keep near to the RH hedge whether or not you are entrained by an electric fence. Walk past several openings in this hedge on the way up and pass Yardgrove Farmhouse over on your right. After a water trough on your left, the fence turns right under a couple of old trees. Follow it, keeping the barns on your left and the hedged field of Yardgrove Farm on your right.

When you arrive in the road outside the barnyard, turn left and cross over instantly to a wide space by a farm gate on the RH side. Up a little bank to the right of this gate, you will find a stile with two Footpath arrows on a post. Go over the stile and turn to follow the LH hedge (340 degrees North), ignoring the other path across the field. Following the hedge, you will have superb views over to your right - and you will probably meet dozens and dozens of rabbits. When I approached Yardgrove Farm, researching for the 1st edition, I came upon a plague of rabbits just after the narrow path with the pool on its left. They seem to have moved from there. They're all in these two fields now.

The church tower over on your right at 30 degrees NE is St Gregory's, Marnhull whilst the wooded hill at 52 degrees ENE is the ever-present Duncliffe Hill.

In 200 yards, there is another Footpath-arrowed stile in the far LH corner which leads into the next field. Cross the stile and aim just to the left of the overhead cable post in the field in front of you (still 340 degrees). Then keep straight on to pass the LH end of the high, tree-filled hedge beyond it. On the corner of this hedge, you will find a post carrying no less than four DCC Footpath arrows. Two paths come from the stile in the hedge over on your left and cross your path to continue either side of this post. Go past the post and keep straight on, slightly leaving the LH hedge, to a double Footpath-arrowed stile near the LH end of the high, facing hedge.

Another path turns right and follows this hedge but keep straight on, over two stiles, the second of which is flanked by upright stone slabs. Bearing right down the next field, angle yourself very slightly away from the bending RH hedge and aim for the stone house with the pool down ahead of you.

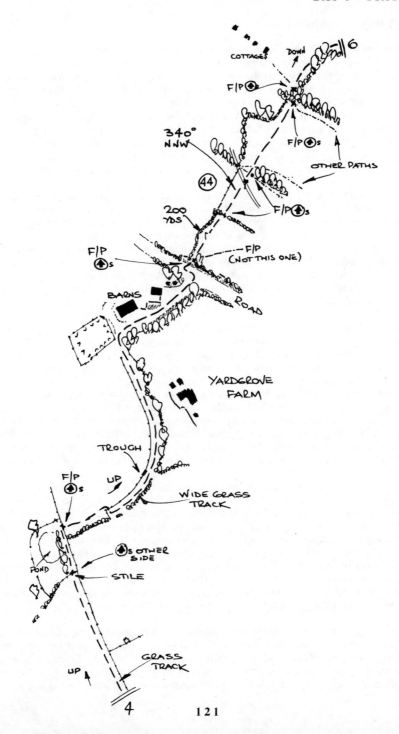

COTTAGES

DOWN

6

F/P s

F/P s

OTHER PATHS

340°
NNW

44

F/P s

200
YDS

F/P
s

F/P
(NOT THIS ONE)

BARNS

ROAD

YARDGROVE
FARM

TROUGH

F/P
s

UP

WIDE GRASS
TRACK

s OTHER
SIDE

POND

STILE

GRASS
TRACK

UP

4

121

DAY 5 - STAGE 6

THROUGH MARNHULL

Follow the hedge down to a kissing gate and two wicket gates which lead you around the duck pond.   Go through the gate in the wooden fence and join the private gravel drive.   Walk up the drive, past the stone house and a few other houses on the RH side, until you emerge onto a busier road just past the farmyard on the LH corner.   Cross the road carefully to a Footpath sign for 'Burton Street 3/4' on the opposite LH corner.   Follow Kentisworth Road to its end and, in the RH corner of the turning area, you will find a short alley between two gardens.   A kissing gate takes you into a field which you walk straight across to another kissing gate (with a Footpath arrow) in the corner facing you.   In the next field, keep to the LH hedge, past a cattle trough and under overhead electric cables, until you reach the end of the hedge and fence.

Stop at this corner as the field slopes down to the left ahead of you.   Take four paces to your right, turn half-right and look down the long hedge over to your right.   You should be able to make out an opening in this hedge (with Duncliffe Hill above it in the distance) and a faint path running from it to where you are standing.   This is an unofficial path because the real Footpath takes a tortuous route down the slope to the trees in the hedge at the bottom and back up the slope to your stile in the top hedge. I can't recommend the short way which passes to the left of an electricity pole but, assuming you have arrived at the Footpath-arrowed stile in the RH hedge, drop into the Sackmore Lane and turn left.

Follow the lane down, past a bench under an ash tree and then, after an easy 1/4 mile between houses and cottages and past the old Congrgational Church on the right, you arrive at a T-junction in Marnhull.   The road to your left is 'Burton Street' as signed at the bungalow estate.   There is a Post Office and a telephone box opposite.   You can't leave Marnhull (which claims to be the largest village in Dorset) without learning a little about it.   In John Hutchins' 'History and Antiquities of the County of Dorset', we find that Marnhull stands "surrounded nearly on three sides by the River Stour which rises from seven wells or springs at what is commonly known as Stourton in Wiltshire but the proper name is StourFont or StourHead".   Marnhull gets its name from "marl hill, a hill of marle as the soil is chiefly a white marl or clay which hardens in air to freestone, easily worked when first dug but gets hard by time".

There are several tales of witches around here but one in particular concerns Mrs Fudge who lived in Marnhull in the early 1900s.   She lived in a cottage at the lower end of Church Hill and, as she stood by her front door one day, she saw a hag-like woman coming down the hill towards her.   Unfortunately, Mrs Fudge laughed at the sight of this strange woman and the hag observed her amusement.   That night in bed, Mrs Fudge felt a weight upon her legs which moved slowly up her body to her chest.   She screamed out in horror and her son burst into her room.   As soon as the door opened, the heavy lump fell off and Mrs Fudge distinctly heard the hag walk down the stairs and out of the door.   Even now, there is an expression used in this area for anyone who has had a nightmare.   They are said to have been "hag-ridden".

At the T-junction, turn right and then immediately left, opposite the stone-pillared porch of Banbury House, into Love Lane.   Follow this leafy lane, past Trooper Farm Cottage, to the first RH bend where you will find a steel, Footpath-arrowed stile next to a farm gate up the bank on your left.   Climb over and, on a bearing of 45 degrees NNE, aim diagonally to your left for the 250 yards-distant gap in the facing hedge.

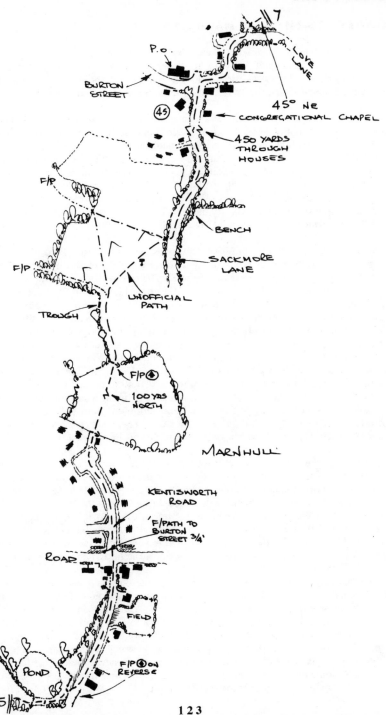

DAY 5 - STAGE 7

MARNHULL TO FIFEHEAD MAGDALEN

Before you leave Marnhull for good, there is more to tell you. The parish church is St Gregory's.   It has an elegant, lofty 15thC tower which is visible for miles in this pastoral landscape.   In the North arcade is a remnant of the 12thC building in a single carved capital whilst the 15thC nave roof and alabaster figures are superb.

Anyway, after the tale of the witch, let's hear one about Marnhull ghosts.   At nearby Todber, a great number of human remains were found during marl quarrying in 1870 and 1871.   At midnight on a certain (un-named) date, a funeral was seen crossing Sackmore Lane from Fillymead to Dunford's.   No mourners attended the ghostly funeral and even the faces of the bearers were hidden beneath the pall which covered the coffin.   The same tale is told of Grove Field, near Nash Court (which once belonged to Catherine Parr, Henry VIII's sixth and surviving wife) which is practically on the same line from Fillymead to Todber.   Nash Court lies just at the end of the lane which you have just left as you climbed over the steel stile.

Now, still walking diagonally for about 250 yards across this first field on the faint 45 degrees NNE path, you arrive at another stile by a gate in the opposite hedge. Follow the 30 degrees NNE direction of the Footpath arrow on the stile across the next field - keeping to the left of the LH of the three big oaks in the middle of the field.   This will bring you to a stile in what appears to be somebody's back garden. It isn't.   Go over the Footpath-arrowed stile and follow the bends and stiles to the wooden steps down into Hains Lane.   Turn right and, just before you reach 'Hains' on your right, go over the arrowed stile in the LH hedge.   Over this stile, aim for the electricity pole which lurks in the hedge near the bottom RH corner of the field.   You will find a stile about 50 yards beyond this pole, on the far side of the deep hedge. Over the stile, bear left across the corner of the next field to a huge lime and a horse-chestnut next to another arrowed stile by a farm gate.   In this peaceful spot opposite the 'Catholic Church of Our Lady', turn left and follow the lane, past the fenced LH field and the RH Meadow Cottage, to the end.   There are gates all around and signposts pointing to 'Fifehead Magdalen 1' and 'Stour Provost 1.1/4'.

Go through the gates onto the gravel driveway of 'Withy Cottage and No. 2' as this is the Public Footpath.   Quietly follow the RH, hedged stone wall to the next stile which leads you into a small field/old orchard.   Keep to the RH hedge and fence to reach the cattle barriers which guard the concrete bridge across the River Stour.   Over the bridge, follow the faint path passing to the left of the electric wires' support post to the LH end of the hedge facing you.   On arrival at the hedge corner, bear very slightly right and aim for the farthest end of this very long field (about 1/2 mile). The gate you will eventually need is 100 yards left of the far RH end of this hedge.

Through this gate, turn instantly right and follow the cut grass path next to the RH hedge, around a left bend and uphill with a ditch between you and the hedge.   At the top, you will find a tarmac track across your path.   Turn right onto the track and go through the gate or the opening.   Immediately turn left and follow the edge of this rising field, around the border of a small copse, keeping to the LH grassy bank.   At the top of this field, turn right and you then come to a gap in the bank.   Turn left through some broken gateposts into the next long, ascending field.   Follow the grassy path alongside the RH hedge, past an opening and up the long field with lovely views to your left, towards the top RH corner .

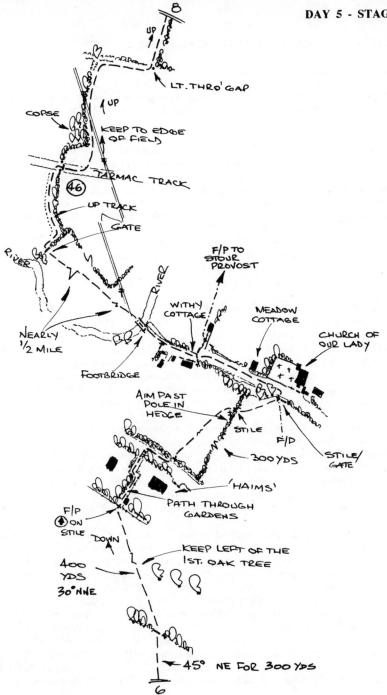

8

UP

LT. THRO' GAP

COPSE

↑ UP

KEEP TO EDGE OF FIELD

TARMAC TRACK

46

UP TRACK

GATE

RIVER

RIVER

F/P TO STOUR PROVOST

NEARLY ½ MILE

WITHY COTTAGE

MEADOW COTTAGE

CHURCH OF OUR LADY

FOOTBRIDGE

AIM PAST POLE IN HEDGE

STILE

F/D

STILE/GATE

300 YDS

'HAIMS'

PATH THROUGH GARDENS

F/P ON STILE DOWN

KEEP LEFT OF THE 1ST. OAK TREE

400 YDS 30° NNE

45° NE FOR 300 YDS

6

125

DAY 5 - STAGE 8

FIFEHEAD MAGDALEN TO STOUR PROVOST

In the top RH corner of this high field, a stile leads into a hollow-way which comes out next to the Old School, Fifehead Magdalen.   Cross over to the Old Post Office side, turn right and follow the road, past stone cottages on your left, to a paddock at the end where a drive goes to the left and a narrow path, to the left of the high stone wall facing you, leads to the Church of St Mary Magdalene.

Fifehead Magdalen takes the second part of its name from the dedication of this church - the first deriving from its old measurement of 'five hides of land' - whilst, in the Domesday Book as *Fifhide*, it boasted two mills and was held by Sir Hugh.   The bright interior of this lovely church contains a magnificent memorial to Sir Richard Newman, who died in 1721, his two wives and three daughters.   Outside, under the great yew, have a look at the inscription on the tomb of Thomas Newman (d 1688):

> *Whilst Tower remaine, or spring my yew,*
> *Here I shall lie as green, young, new,*
> *.....news to us good times shall bring,*
> *One swallow doth not make the spring.*

Back outside the churchyard, past the iron gates, turn down the lane and go past the stile and gate on the LH bend which share a 'West Stour' sign .   Keep on down for about 100 yards to the next LH gate in the hedge.   Here the sign reads 'Footpath. Stour Provost 1/2'.   Through the gate, keep to the LH hedge as the field drops down about 250 yards to a LH sleeper bridge and a Footpath-arrowed stile.   Go over the stile and you will find yourself in a high field with marsh grass near the top.   Take two paces straight on into this high field and look down (at 75 degrees ENE), aiming for the stile in the fence in the far bottom corner, near to the River Stour.

Over this arrowed stile, turn right and follow the edge of the Stour for about 1/4 mile. Towards the end of this fine riverside stroll, there are some lovely views of the sluice gates and pool of Stour Provost Mill on the other side.   Go past the 'Private Fishing' sign and the arrowed post by the gate and cross the bridge.   On the other side, turn right to the next gate onto a path over the sluice gates where you now pass through private land.   The plaque on the mill wall commemorates the restoration of the mill, after more than 60 years disuse, by Derek Llewelyn who used it to generate electricity.

Now, go through the Footpath-arrowed wicket gate on your left which brings you onto the garden lawn.   Walk left of the stone workshop, between trees and past a bench, to a stile in the wire fence and go over into the steeply sloping field on the other side.   Head diagonally right up this field - just missing the top RH end of a clump of trees - to the top by a low, stone barn.   Go over the stile by the gate and follow the wide, grassy track with various stone walls on either side.   Bearing right, the track rises to become tarmac and emerges onto a T-junction.   Turn right and stroll up into Stour Provost.   The first grassy path on your left before Brookside Cottage leads to the lovely 14th/15thC church of St Michael which was restored in 1838.   It has a fine big lych gate and, inside, it has a lovely chancel ceiling, elegant lancet windows on the South side and a "striking clock with no face" which was built by William Monk of Berwick St John (a village visited on 'The Cranborne Chase Path').

Now, return to continue down the shady lane past the junction where you came in.

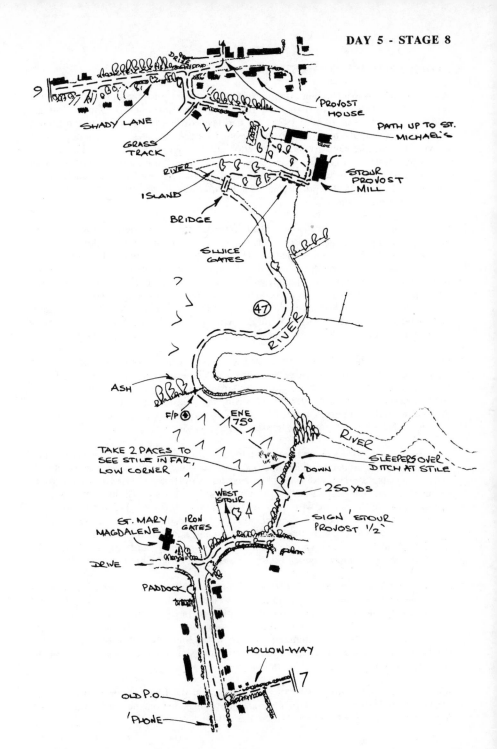

SHADY LANE

GRASS TRACK

'PROVOST HOUSE

PATH UP TO ST. MICHAEL'S

ISLAND

RIVER

BRIDGE

SLUICE GATES

STOUR PROVOST MILL

47

RIVER

ASH

F/P ⊕

ENE 75°

TAKE 2 PACES TO SEE STILE IN FAR, LOW CORNER

RIVER

SLEEPERS OVER DITCH AT STILE

DOWN

250 YDS

WEST STOUR

SIGN 'STOUR PROVOST ½'

ST. MARY MAGDALENE

IRON GATES

DRIVE

PADDOCK

HOLLOW-WAY

OLD P.O

'PHONE

127

DAY 5 - STAGE 9

STOUR PROVOST TO WEST STOUR

As you wander down the lane, there's just a little more information to be imparted. Most of Stour Provost was owned by the Provost and scholars of Kings College, Cambridge from about 1450 to 1925. It had been owned before then by the French monastery of Priaulx but, during one of our frequent disputes with France, Stour Provost was seized and given as an endowment to Kings College. During the enclosures of 1624, a Chancery decree maintained that the villages "1300 acres of large pasture ground or waste....is used to small profit. By division and enclosure it would yield much greater profit to all tenants *and also to the Provost, fellows and scholars at Kings College".*

Now, continue down the steep sided, shady lane past several attractive stone cottages and the really pretty garden of Rowlands on your left. A little further down the lane at Riversdale Farm take the signed 'Pedestrians' diversion around the right of the farmyard. A gravel track, cut into the slopes on your right, leads you on into a hedged farm track. Take the first left gate, down an angled dip, into a large field. On a bearing of 300 degrees NW, aim for the far, low down, RH corner of the field at the bottom end of the long hedge which faces you. You should see a collection of gates and a bald, earthy patch. After 1/4 mile, when you reach that corner, you will find a gateway bridging a small stream which leads you into the next very large field.

Stop and scan the far end of this next field for a distant, wood-railed footbridge. A faint, meandering path (at approx 280 degrees WNW) leads you there, keeping the RH hedge several yards away for 600 yards. Arriving at the footbridge, with steps and stiles at either end, cross the Stour. This is a very pleasant spot with water lilies and dragonflies in the summer. I saw a 15 inch trout swimming under the bridge in early summer. I don't know how that translates into pounds.

Now, stop on the other side and search up the steeply sloping field. You need to aim just right of a gable-ended cottage (the one with trees and a red-roofed barn on its LH end). The big stone house on its right is the 'Ship Inn'. For the increasingly technical, this is 320 degrees NW. As you climb up this steep field, you should be coming closer to the double wire fence on your right. 100 yards before the cottage at the top, there are two Footpath-arrowed stiles and a sleeper bridge spanning the ditch between two wire fences. In the next field, turn half left and aim straight for the Ship Inn (340 degrees). This leads you to a stile, 20 yards towards the road from the corner of the wooden fence which borders the car park of the Ship Inn, West Stour.

The 1st edition of 'The Stour Valley Path' suggested that you should go in and ask why it's called the Ship Inn even though it's so far from the sea. They may be a bit fed up with being asked by now, so why not just pop in for a little refreshment - after all, it's less than 4 miles to the end of your Day. Incidentally, the Royal Commission for Historic Monuments says about the Ship Inn - "West Stour (8), two-storeyed, with coursed rubble and ashlar walls, and slate-covered roofs. It is of the early 19th century".

Right, on the road again. Past the inn, turn round the first LH corner into Church Street. Cottages called The Triangle and Sunnybank stand on the right as you stroll towards a bench and a telephone box on the left.

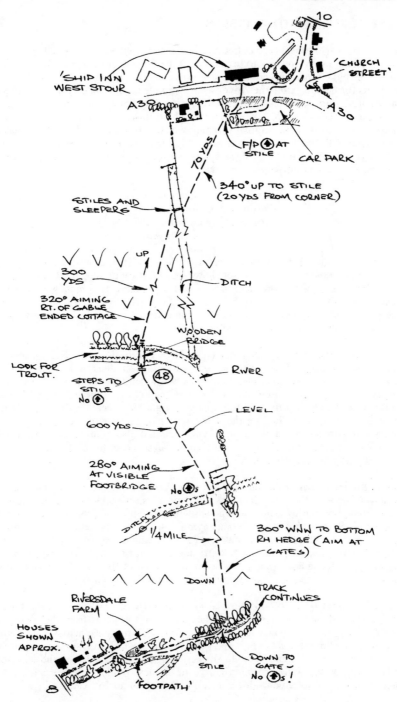

10

'SHIP INN'
WEST STOUR

'CHURCH
STREET'

A30

A30

F/P AT
STILE

CAR PARK

340° UP TO STILE
(20 YDS FROM CORNER)

70 YDS

STILES AND
SLEEPERS

UP

300
YDS

DITCH

320° AIMING
RT. OF GABLE
ENDED COTTAGE

WOODEN
BRIDGE

LOOK FOR
TROUT.

STEPS TO
STILE
No ⊕

48

RIVER

LEVEL

600 YDS

280° AIMING
AT VISIBLE
FOOTBRIDGE

No ⊕s

DITCH

¼ MILE

300° WNW TO BOTTOM
RH HEDGE (AIM AT
GATES)

DOWN

TRACK
CONTINUES

RIVERSDALE
FARM

HOUSES
SHOWN
APPROX.

DOWN TO
GATE –
No ⊕s!

STILE

8

'FOOTPATH'

129

DAY 5 - STAGE 10

WEST STOUR TO STOUR FIELDS

This is a good spot to rest for a coffee and a sandwich - unless you stopped at the Ship Inn.   Passing pretty cottages to left and right, the high wall of Ashley House on the left and the old Chapel on your right, you arrive at the Village Hall on the left.   A few yards further on, after the driveway to Church Farm Estate, you will find the Church of St Mary in the high churchyard on your left.   St Mary's (picture on p.132) is unusual for Dorset in that the tower was rebuilt during restoration work in 1840 whilst the only part of the original structure which still remains is the 13thC chancel. A memorial in the chapel is worth noting.   The inscription to the memory of Martin Meateyard who died in 1733, aged 63, is a salutary reminder of why we're out enjoying this wonderful fresh air so much:

> *Behold all you that here pass by*
> *This house of clay wherein I ly.*
> *Your mortal state behold and see*
> *For as I am so must you be.*

In 1541-1542, the 33rd year of the reign of Henry VIII, the muster roll of fit and fighting men in the County of Dorset shows that West Stour supported seven archers and billmen (men with bows and arrows *and* billhooks), two men who were just archers, four who possessed only billhooks and one who even had a suit of armour. Out of a current population of less than two hundred souls, I wonder how many archers or men with billhooks could be found here today.

Now, opposite the church on the LH bend in the lane, turn down the RH, narrow path signed 'Harpitts Bridge 1' and descend between cottage gardens into a shady hollow-way.   Follow it to the other end where a new wooden fence with a Footpath arrow directs you sharply left to go over a stile and keep close to the LH trees.   Don't venture onto the tarmac drive coming from your right but, where the drive bends right again, keep straight on through the new wood and go over the stile in its far LH corner into a field which slopes away to your right into the Stour valley.   Keep close to the wooden fence and the fir trees on your left and go over the next stile by the gate ahead of you into yet another field.

Standing in the corner of the gate and the wire fence on the other side, walk straight ahead (in line with this short fence at 338 degrees NNW) and keep up high in this field.   Some new fences were under construction as I prepared this revision so there may be a whole new wire fence accompanying you across this field now.   Anyway, aim just past the LH end of the new, fenced wood which faces you and you'll find a stile with a painted arrow on it.   Sadly, it doesn't point the right way and you can't yet see the next stile because it's way down the bottom of the next field which drops away ahead of you and also slopes down into the valley on your right.

This is how you find it.   From Point X on the map (here), look beyond the brow of this field to find the RH end of the high hedge, about 150 yards from the bottom LH corner (20 degrees NE).   There may be a temporary electric fence across your path en route but just climb straight over it and keep aiming down to that spot.   On arrival, you will find twin stiles and a single sleeper over the stream between the wire fence and the hedge at the bottom of this field.   In the next field, there is a gate on your immediate left but brace yourself for a climb, straight up for 230 yards.

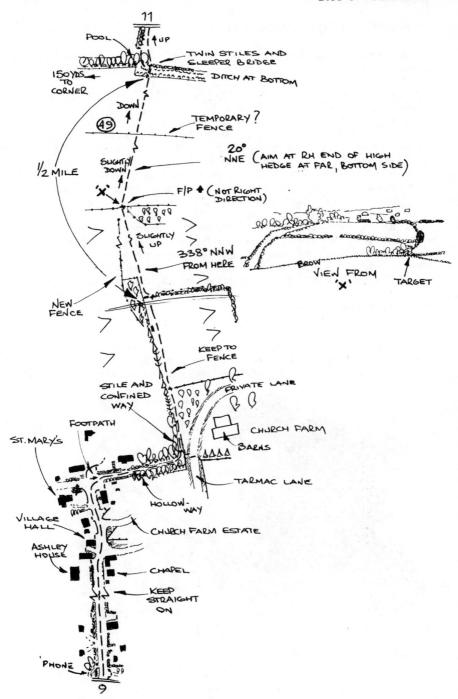

DAY 5 - STAGE 11

STOUR FIELDS TO NATIONS ROAD

Follow the hedge up this steep field to the stile and gate in the top LH corner but don't miss the lovely views across the fields and the Stour valley on your right.

Take care in this next field as the way out is just as difficult.   Follow the LH hedge until it bends away left towards the gate in the top LH corner.   Bear right and look along the facing hedge for 50 yards downhill, searching in the thick hedge for an opening which hides a stile.   Actually, due to the depth of the hedge, there are two stiles.   On the other side, the field slopes away to the river at its foot.   Find a line (354 degrees/almost due North) which aims for the bridge down on a far bend of the Stour - on a line which shows some barns above the bridge on the horizon.   Start walking down the changing gradients of this undulating field, heading between the first oak and the second willow, diagonally right, down in front of you.

At the bottom, join some cattle tracks alongside the river until you reach the bridge. Go past the bridge and through the gap in the far corner of this field (possibly with a feeble stream running across your path) into a smaller area in which cows are seen to congregate.   Turn sharp left, away from the river and alongside the wire fence, to a stile onto a tarmac road.   Turn right in the road and, due to a lack of verges or footpaths, you now have an easy mile of road walking, but it's less than two miles altogether to the end of today's excursion.   Just follow the road between high banks, hedges and fine old trees to a fenced drive to Wool House on your right.

After Wool House and the lane which turns off to your left, go under some large beech, oak, copper beech and ash trees which overhang the road from left to right and keep going, with the Stour sunken in the fields on your right, not far below the road level.

St Mary's Church, West Stour - On Stage 10

132

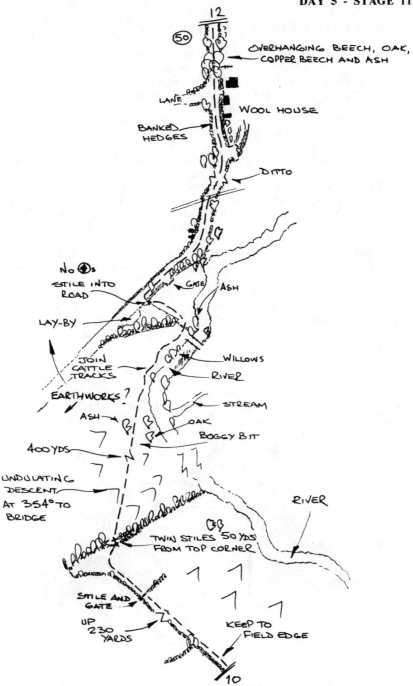

12

50

OVERHANGING BEECH, OAK,
COPPER BEECH AND ASH

LANE

WOOL HOUSE

BANKED
HEDGES

DITTO

No 4 s
STILE INTO
ROAD

GATE

ASH

LAY-BY

JOIN
CATTLE
TRACKS

WILLOWS

RIVER

EARTHWORKS?

STREAM

ASH

OAK

BOGGY BIT

400 YDS

UNDULATING
DESCENT
AT 354° TO
BRIDGE

RIVER

TWIN STILES 50 YDS
FROM TOP CORNER

STILE AND
GATE

UP
230
YARDS

KEEP TO
FIELD EDGE

10

133

DAY 5 - STAGE 12

NATIONS ROAD TO THORNGROVE LODGE

Past a long, stone cottage called Nations, past Walnut Tree Farm and arriving at a small fenced wood, all on the left, the road bends left and goes under a very high, brick and stone railway arch. Turn off right here and keep straight on where a small stream runs under your lane to join the Stour on your right. (The flat-topped wall on the right is quite a handy seat for you to finish off your last sandwich). The signpost points to 'Eccliffe' and, in a few yards, you meet the real Stour again as it runs under a cattle bridge just off the road on your right.

The railway embankment accompanies you behind the hedge on your left but gets further and further away. Eventually, when the lane turns right by a cottage at Eccliffe, turn sharp left past a Footpath arrow post and go through a farm gate next to the cottage and into a rising field between the lane and the embankment. Follow the wooden fence on your right and you will find an opening. Go through it and bear diagonally left towards a Footpath-arrowed stile in the fence alongside the bank - minding the well grating en route. Over the stile, go through the tunnel under the railway line and, past another Footpath arrow post, out into the field on the other side. If it's of any interest, a train runs overhead at precisely 12:21 pm in the week.

Aiming at a distant, many-gabled lodge (355 degrees N), cross the field and go over the horse jump/stile in the wire fence into the next field. There are a barn, stables and a red-brick house over on your left as you cross this field. Here, follow the hedge on your right past a couple of large oaks to a stile in the far RH corner and go over into the last field before a road.

Old Wyke Brewery - On Stage 13

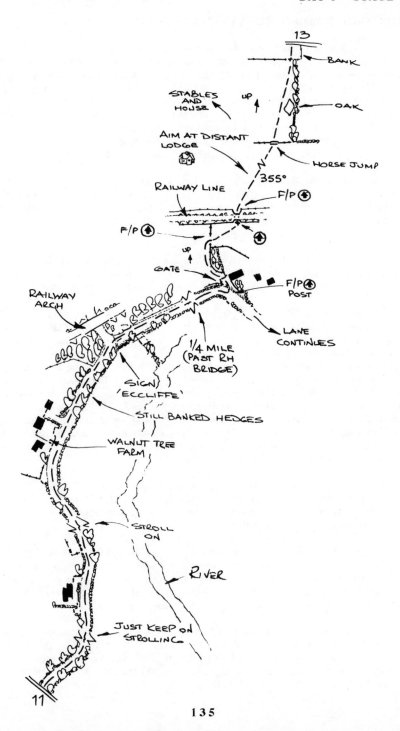

13

BANK

STABLES
AND
HOUSE

UP

OAK

AIM AT DISTANT
LODGE

HORSE JUMP

355°

RAILWAY LINE

F/P

F/P

F/P

UP

GATE

F/P
POST

RAILWAY
ARCH

LANE
CONTINUES

¼ MILE
(PAST RH
BRIDGE)

SIGN
'ECCLIFFE'

STILL BANKED HEDGES

WALNUT TREE
FARM

STROLL
ON

RIVER

JUST KEEP ON
STROLLING

11

THORNGROVE LODGE TO WYKE CROSSROADS

Over the Footpath-arrowed stile next to the farm gate onto the road, cross over and go up the wide, tree-lined driveway opposite, signed for 'Thorngrove Centre'. After the Lodge and the second big tree in the RH grass verge, look for the Footpath arrow post and the stile in the wire fence. Climb over into the parkland and cross straight over to another stile in the high, tree-filled hedge opposite. This stile leads into a narrow wood with an exit stile on the other side leading into an open field. In this field, there is a new rest home or block of flats over the RH fence and Duncliffe Hill seems quite close, straight ahead. Beyond this field are the outermost dwellings of Wyke and Gillingham but the expansion appears to be approaching fast.

Aim to the right of the overhead cable post slightly to your left. You can see the Old Brewery towers on your left as you diagonally cross this field (at 18 degrees NNE). This path is well worn as it comes from the estate but, before you reach the stile which leads into the houses, turn off to the left onto another path (352 degrees -nearly N) which leads to an opening in a high hedge.

From this field, you should be able to make out a highly significant landmark. Away in the distance, you can see the bulk of Alfred's Tower. This stands close to the head of the valley in which the River Stour rises - journey's end at Six Wells Bottom.

In this next large field of varying widths, follow the line of the houses on your right (and cross another popular path) for about 300 yards until you arrive in the far RH corner at yet another stile - the last today. Over the stile, between a wooden fence on the left and a hedge on the right, behind both of which are now several houses, follow the path - now a tarmac lane - all the way to join the B3081. On the way, you will pass 'The Buffalo' on your right. A charging buffalo was the Trade Mark of the original Wyke Brewery which was founded about 1760 and which continued brewing until the late 1960s by which time it had been taken over by Hall and Woodhouse of Blandford Forum. At the end of this lane, which you will see is called Lydford Lane, the old brewery is the big brick building which stands down on your left on the B3081 (picture on p.134) but its remaining buildings and land have been converted into flats, an antiques store and a housing estate.

All that Rev Hutchins tells us about Wyke is that it is a "hamlet 1/2 mile NW from Gillingham" and that it is "named after Richard de Wyke - 2EdIII" (1329). By the way, if you're 'not from round these parts', the G in Gillingham is pronounced as a G not as a J (unlike its namesake in Kent).

The road opposite, Pound Lane, is the starting point for the last leg. If you're going into Gillingham - turn right and keep straight on past the traffic lights at the T-junction with the new by-pass. You cross over a small river on the way. This is the Stour but the wider river which runs through the other end of town is Shreen Water. The two of them meet up South of Gillingham High Street.

King John built a hunting palace here in 1199, the ramparts and foundations of which still exist 1/2 mile East of the town at King's Court. The Church of the Blessed Virgin, St Mary was restored in 1838-39 whilst its remaining 14thC chancel is five bays long. The tower is blessed with typical Somerset tracery - a sure sign that we are only 2.1/2 miles from the county boundary.

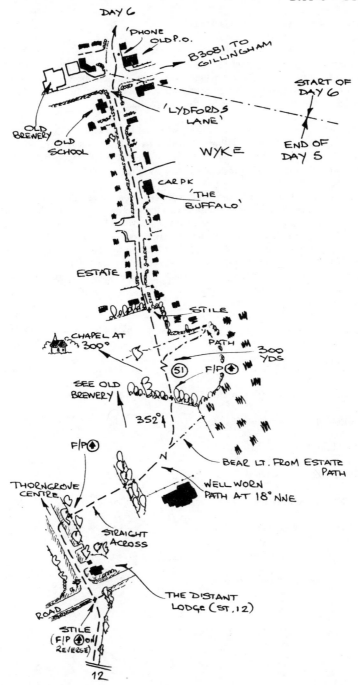

DAY 6

'PHONE
OLD P.O.

B3081 TO
GILLINGHAM

START OF
DAY 6

'LYDFORDS
LANE'

OLD
BREWERY

OLD
SCHOOL

WYKE

END OF
DAY 5

CAR PK
'THE
BUFFALO'

ESTATE

STILE

CHAPEL AT
300°

PATH

300
YDS

51   F/P

SEE OLD
BREWERY

352°

F/P

N

BEAR LT. FROM ESTATE
PATH

THORNGROVE
CENTRE

WELL WORN
PATH AT 18° NNE

STRAIGHT
ACROSS

THE DISTANT
LODGE (ST.12)

ROAD

STILE
(F/P ON
REVERSE)

12

DAY 6 - INTRODUCTION

WYKE CROSSROADS TO STOURTON

The shortage of inns and churches on this final Stage of 'The New Stour Valley Path' is amply compensated by the beautiful scenery, the woods, the hills, the lakes and the valleys which have been waiting to enchant everybody on this approach to the source of the River Stour.   Actually, one inn, one church *and* a tea-room are waiting for you at the very end - for your celebrations in Stourton village.

Day 5's route wandered along an undulating and meandering path as the young River Stour wended its casual way from village to village over the Dorset plains.   The final Stage leads through more lovely hamlets and ancient woodland with huge oaks, beeches and chestnuts in deep valleys and over gentle hills.

From Wyke crossroads where you departed from the scene at the end of Day 5, easy walking along country lanes leads you quickly to the ancient hamlet of Silton - where there *is* a lovely little church - and, after you have crossed both the new and the old A303s into Bourton, another stone-built hamlet soon follows.   This is Pen Selwood, from where it is a particularly delightful 2.1/2 miles to the valley of Six Wells Bottom - your El Dorado where the springs bubble from beneath the dry valley floor into medieval fish-ponds.   Here, the pure fresh infant River Stour begins its long journey to the English Channel at Christchurch.

	STAGE	MILES	TOTAL MILES
1	Wyke Crossroads to Milton on Stour	1	52.50
2	Milton on Stour to Silton Hill	.75	53.25
3	Silton Hill to Stocking Bridge	.75	54
4	Stocking Bridge to Bourton	1	55
5	Bourton to Pen Selwood	.50	55.50
6	Pen Selwood to Harcourt Farm	.50	56
7	Harcourt Farm to Top Lane	1	57
8	Top Lane to Six Wells Bottom	1	58
9	Six Wells Bottom to Stourton	1.50	59.50

WYKE CROSSROADS TO STOURTON

Summer House, Stourhead

Stourhead House

DAY 6 - STAGE 1

WYKE CROSROADS TO MILTON ON STOUR

Return to the cross-roads from whence you departed to your rest and walk down Pound Lane past the post box on your left. Between the hedge on your left and bungalows on your right, keep on until you arrive at a T-junction at the end. A vast housing estate has been built behind the bungalows and expansion of Gillingham appears to be gathering momentum. I mention this as it may affect the next part of the route sooner or later.

Cross over the road to a steel gate which bridges the space between two driveways and leads onto a short, wide grass track. Through the Footpath-arrowed gate, go straight on to a stile next to another gate. Over this stile, follow the direction of the Footpath arrow - a little right of straight on - to join a hedge as it runs down into the far RH corner of the field.

Here, another arrowed stile leads into another field with tractor tracks joining you from the right, behind the hedge. Aim to walk past the two overhead cables' posts where the hedge begins again after the open space. When the electricity authorities replaced the old stanchion with these posts, they seem to have taken the Footpath arrows away with them. However, keep to the 140 yards long hedge until it suddenly stops and then cross the open field, bearing to your left at 352 degrees N for about 300 yards, until you find a farm gate with an adjacent stile in the outer hedge. Over the stile, you emerge onto a track junction with a tarmac lane. There are two Footpath arrows on the outside, one of which points back to your path whilst the other points up the track to your right. Join the road and, with grass verges both sides, begin an easy stroll, keeping to the right.

You soon arrive in Milton on Stour, listed as *Miltetone* in the Domesday Book. Before the Conquest, the manor was owned by Godmund, King Harold's thane, but it then passed to William de Falaise. By Richard II's time (late 14thC) the village was known as Milton juxta (*near to*) Gillingham to distinguish it from all of the other Miltons in Dorset. The church of Saints Simon and Jude, which stands on the B3095 and is some way from our immediate route, is Victorian - built in 1868 in the Early-English style.

Keep on, past the first turning where the sign welcomes you to 'Milton On Stour', some houses on the left and some older stone cottages on your right, until you come to Milton Garden Plants, a subsidiary of Milton Farm whose barns and outbuildings are next on the right.

Incidentally, the young River Stour runs parallel with this road, about 400 yards across to your right, but there are no Rights of Way through the farmland for a while. Never mind. The next couple of miles are very easy and your stroll through working farm country will leave you refreshed and exhilarated. You'll soon catch up with the little river and you'll be playing Pooh-sticks before you know it.

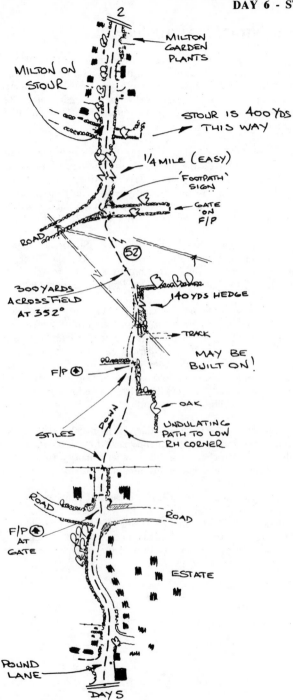

2

MILTON GARDEN PLANTS

MILTON ON STOUR

STOUR IS 400 YDS THIS WAY

¼ MILE (EASY)

'FOOTPATH' SIGN

GATE ON F/P

ROAD

57

300 YARDS ACROSS FIELD AT 352°

140 YDS HEDGE

TRACK

MAY BE BUILT ON!

F/P ⊕

OAK

STILES

DOWN

UNDULATING PATH TO LOW RH CORNER

ROAD

ROAD

F/P ⊕ AT GATE

ESTATE

POUND LANE

DAY 5

DAY 6 - STAGE 2

MILTON ON STOUR TO SILTON HILL

Before the farmyards, you cross over a bridge under which a wide stream flows from the left and disappears under a stone barn on the right en route for the Stour.   After the high trees lining the estate on your left, you arrive at a T-junction with a stone-piered entrance to a fine house on the LH corner.   Turn left.   The right turn takes you on to Milton on Stour church but it's quite a long way and it stands on the other side of the busy B3095.

So, going left on the lane called 'Pierston Fields', between banked hedges on both sides at first, you soon pass the paddocks and the tennis courts which belong to the aforementioned fine house.   This is easy walking, especially after the fields and innumerable stiles of Day 5's Stages, and you can really feel journey's end coming on apace.   Following the lane, past a couple of huge horse-chestnuts on the left and Whistley House on the right, you soon arrive at Pierston Farm on your right.

Pierston formerly shared a tithing with Milton on Stour and consisted of "a manor, a hamlet and a farm" and, according to Rev Hutchins, "the River Stour abounds with trout, running through the centre of the premises".   There were certainly some in the river below the Ship Inn at West Stour but Pierston is probably too far upstream now.

There is a wide verge on the right as you ascend slightly with open fields on your left and hedged fields on your right.   Reaching the top of the rise, there are still open fields on the left whilst rows of trees show where streams run in the valley bottoms on either side.   The one on the right carries the junior River Stour.   As you descend again, with the RH verge having been replaced by a ditch, a bank and a wire fence, you will see a farm gate and a big, old oak perched on top of the bank.   Once upon a time, this tree very kindly sheltered me from a sudden, fierce downpour which had crept up on me from behind.

It was at this point - on the last Day - that I suddenly thought of a good reason for *not* walking from sea to source.   The sun might well be shining from behind as you walk from South to North but changes in the weather usually arrive from the South West as well and you can't see the clouds building up behind you.

Down the lane, you pass an open barn on the left from where you can see Alfred's Tower again and, on your forward right, the village of Zeals.   Then a turning goes left to 'Whistley Farm and Whistley Water'.   Keep straight on down and up for another 200 yards and, opposite a gated entrance to a barn behind the hedge, another lane turns off to your right at the foot of a shady, ascending and steep-banked section of the lane.

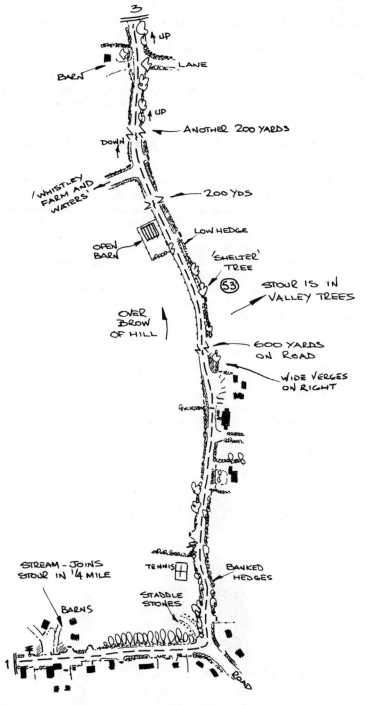

3

↑ UP

LANE

BARN

↑ UP

← ANOTHER 200 YARDS

DOWN

'WHISTLEY FARM AND WATERS'

← 200 YDS

LOW HEDGE

OPEN BARN

'SHELTER' TREE

(53)

STOUR IS IN VALLEY TREES

OVER BROW OF HILL

← 600 YARDS ON ROAD

WIDE VERGES ON RIGHT

STREAM - JOINS STOUR IN ¼ MILE

TENNIS

BANKED HEDGES

STADDLE STONES

BARNS

1

ROAD

143

DAY 6 - STAGE 3

SILTON HILL TO STOCKING BRIDGE

Carry on up the hedged and banked lane, now with overhanging trees, to the top of the rise.   You are now arriving in the hamlet of Silton with the barns and yards of Manor Farm at the top on your right.   The area around the farmhouse and its stables has been beautifully landscaped with new trees and trimmed grass open areas on the right and there remains a really ancient, gnarled tree right by the side of the road.   In 'Dorset Upalong and Downalong', it says "At Silton, the Court leet was held under an ancient oak tree, the trunk of which measured 38 feet in circumference".   This *must* be it.   Listed in the Domesday Book as *Seltone*, this hamlet, too, was given to William de Falaise.

Over the stone field wall on your left, there are some fine farmland views and, continuing down the lane, the church of St Nicholas, appears over on the right above a long, stone wall.   A few paces after a hedged cottage on the right, the church entrance is found just around the corner of the garden hedge.   The present building dates from Norman times but it was altered in the 12th/13thC and the tower is 15thC. A huge restoration took place in 1869 under the Rector and Patron, William Percy. When you go inside, you can't fail to notice the huge monument to Sir Hugh Wyndham, Justice of the Common Pleas under Oliver Cromwell *and* Charles II.   John Hutchins described the church's fine setting thus - "It stands on a knoll in the midst of a rich and well-wooded country; and the views from the churchyard are peculiarly pleasing".   You really should go and have a look.   It has a comfortable seat in the churchyard as well

Just a little further down the lane, stone piers and iron gates on your right lead to a large, stone house with a lovely garden and, continuing along Church Road, you pass Taylor Hayes cottages on the left and a continuous high hedge on the right.   After the banked hedges descend, a lane turns off left to 'Feltham Farm Only'.   Keep straight on and, where the road goes over a small stream or ditch, just keep on going - this is Stocking Bridge.   Shortly, another lane turns off to the right signed 'Ford. 400 yards'.

St Nicholas' Church, Silton

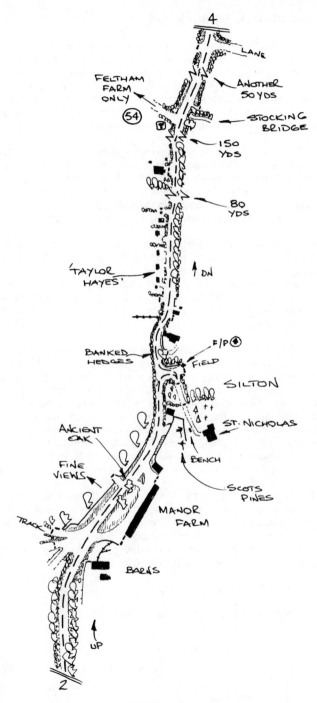

4

LANE

FELTHAM
FARM
ONLY

ANOTHER
50 YDS

54

STOCKING
BRIDGE

150
YDS

80
YDS

DN

TAYLOR
HAYES'

F/P

FIELD

BANKED
HEDGES

SILTON

ANCIENT
OAK

ST. NICHOLAS

FINE
VIEWS

BENCH

SCOTS
PINES

TRACK

MANOR
FARM

BARNS

UP

2

STOCKING BRIDGE TO BOURTON

Soon, a right bend brings you to a slate-roofed stone house, the Village Hall and a telephone box on the left, just opposite a cattle grid in the entrance to Stroud Cottage on your right. Turn left before the LH house onto a really rough track with grass up the middle. It sports a Footpath sign to 'Bourton 1/2'. On your left up this track is Stroud Common, now Stroud Park, which, before the Enclosure Act, provided free grazing for a few tenants who lived close by. On my final check, I'll swear there was an emu watching me over the gateway - but don't tell anybody.

At the end of the 100 yards long track, go through the gate and cross the small field, aiming for the far LH corner where the high hedge meets a wooden fence across your path. Go over the stile and walk slowly down the paved steps in the embankment to the busy A303 Bourton By-Pass at the bottom. Take great care crossing as this is alien territory to pedestrians, especially 54 miles into a country walk. Whilst the picture on p.148 shows it completely empty, it isn't always thus.

Safely negotiating the barrier in the central reservation, cross to the fence and steps back up the opposite embankment to a stile at the top. Over the stile, you will find a small gate on your right and another Footpath-arrowed stile on your left. Ignore them both and plough down the (possibly overgrown with nettles) hedged pathway which is facing you. A RH fenced ditch and a high, banked LH hedge accompany your fight down this path until you emerge at a junction with a wide track from East View Farm on your left.

There is a gate into the field which is almost opposite you but bear right, away from it for a few paces. Here, you will find a pair of Footpath arrows. Turn to the LH stile - right on the corner - which leads onto a path which runs along the high RH bank of the field that faced you when you emerged from the path. Enclosed variously by odd trees scattered about the bank and a fence at the foot of the bank on your left, keep straight on until the path drops down off the bank. Continue in the same direction until you are disgorged onto a wider grass track with some houses on your left and the hedge on your right. At the top of this grassy drive, you find the old A303 running quietly through Bourton. There is a petrol station just down the road to your right if you need provisions. You now have a choice of two ways for the next 1/4 mile.

THE OLD ORIGINAL ROUTE: Cross over to the pavement opposite and turn left, passing a bus shelter on your way to Mill Lane which is next on the right. On the reservation opposite the shelter - centrally in Breach Close - there is a huge boulder with a commemorative plaque which was erected by the much-relieved Celebration Committee of Bourton when the by-pass finally saved them and the neighbouring village of Zeals from the thundering traffic.

Turn right up the aforementioned Mill Lane.

THE SECOND CHOICE: For a short re-acquaintance with the young River Stour, turn right and go down the A303.

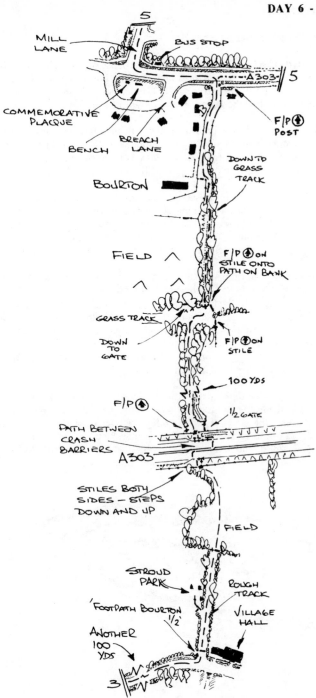

5

MILL
LANE

BUS STOP

A 303 5

COMMEMORATIVE
PLACQUE

F/P Post

BENCH

BREACH
LANE

DOWN TO
GRASS
TRACK

BOURTON

FIELD

F/P ON
STILE ONTO
PATH ON BANK

GRASS TRACK

DOWN
TO
GATE

F/P ON
STILE

100 YDS

F/P

½ GATE

PATH BETWEEN
CRASH
BARRIERS

A303

STILES BOTH
SIDES — STEPS
DOWN AND UP

FIELD

STROUD
PARK

ROUGH
TRACK

FOOTPATH BOURTON
½

VILLAGE
HALL

ANOTHER
100
YDS

3

DAY 6 - STAGE 5

BOURTON TO PEN MILL

THE OLD ORIGINAL ROUTE: Passing New Close on the right and Mill Rise on the left, continue down the high-hedged lane, passing houses up on the right and Mill Cottage on the left, until you arrive at a T-junction with an iron fence opposite. Turn sharp left and follow the hedge around a tight hairpin.

THE NEW ROUTE: At the bottom of the hill, turn left into Bridge Street. The river is over the stone wall on your right.   Indeed, it flows under the bridge by the 'Old Toll Bridge Cottage'.   A few yards further, you can see it coming across the field from Bourton Mill.   Follow the road, past Mill Lane coming down from your left.

EVERYBODY: Go through the second gate up the hill which leads you onto an uphill, gravel track with grass up the middle, between wire fences.   It is signposted 'to Pen Mill 1/2' and overlooks the Mill Factory down on your right.   Bourton Mill once employed 200 people in a foundry and in the manufacture of sacks.   It was powered by a huge 60ft diameter water wheel - one of the biggest in the country.

With a hedge joining you from your high left, continue to where the track bears right towards Farcombe Hall and Old Charlie Young's Cottage.   Climb over a stile in the wooden fence near a gate to the left and follow the clear grass track across the sloping field.   Arriving at a kissing gate, underneath a most unfriendly holly tree, squirm carefully into the next field.   Follow the grass track, uphill and then level, as the field rises quite steeply and unevenly on your left and drops away down a bracken-filled bank on the right.   Dropping down a short, grassy gully you come to an old kissing gate next to another farm gate in the banked hedge.

Through here, keep to the raised path with marshy ground on either side as it drops to a gate and stile in the hedge and fence at the bottom.   Over the stile, walk alongside the pond and above the steep, wooded valley on your right. Follow the path into a hedged drive and out to its junction with a tarmac lane.   The road past the stone cottage with a mounting block down on your right leads to the Stour but you have to cross over the road and go between the barn and the garage.

A303 before Bourton - On Stage 4

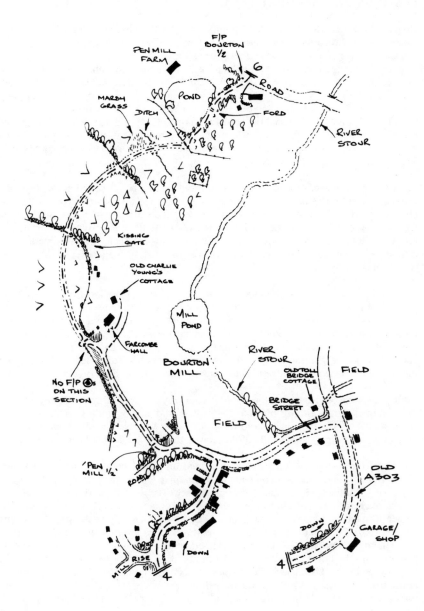

DAY 6 - STAGE 6

PEN MILL TO HARCOURT FARM

Go past the Footpath signpost to 'Coombe Street 1/2 and Pear Ash 3/4' and up the narrow path between the stone walls of two barns.   Now, with a wire fence on your right, you arrive at a wicket gate into a private yard.   Keep round to the right and go through the Footpath-arrowed kissing gate next to the farm gate ahead of you.   Go up the steep bank, past a big tree in the embankment to your left and with a wide, grass valley stretching away to your left.   You are now in a large field with a steep drop down to woods and a hedge on your right.   The River Stour flows through these mixed woods on its way to feed the headwater pond of Bourton Mill which you passed earlier.   On a recent visit, my eye was caught by a movement on a nearby tree trunk below this path.   A pair of tree-creepers were busy doing - well, what do you expect? That's right, creeping up the trees.

The path is now easier to find than it once was.   Must be all the Stour Valley Path walkers.   Aim for the far end of the cottage garden hedge up ahead of you.   Passing about 15 yards to the right of the nearest corner of the garden (which has an arrow on it), you arrive at a stile in the far LH corner of the field.   Go over the Footpath-arrowed stile into a narrow, gravel alley for a few yards and then, where the path veers off left around the back of the gardens, go over the stile in the RH fence into a field which drops away into the valley facing you.

Look straight across the valley and you will see a stile in the far, tree-filled hedge. Aiming at a point about 20 yards to the right of the copse in the bottom of the valley, (28 degrees NNE) you will be able to cross the stream in Coombe Bottom on some rough stepping-stones.   Then walk straight up the steep slope on the far side and you'll find the stile in the trees bordering the field.   Go over the stile into the woods and follow the meandering path - ignoring the one which goes off left and upwards - down to the wooden footbridge which spans the infant River Stour again.

Collect a couple of twigs from the floor on your way.   Then linger awhile to watch the young river wandering off into the woods and maybe indulge in a game of 'Poohsticks'.   Handy hint - avoid the slack water to the right of the stream when dropping your twig.   The middle of the flow is the best place - but keep it to yourself.

Then carry on up the steep, narrow and hedged-in, gravel path with an embankment on the right at first, until you come out onto a tarmac lane with a Footpath pointer at your exit.   Turn left up the lane, passing a gate to Harcourt Farm down on your left. As the road makes a hairpin to the right past a wooden fence and a gate in the RH corner, turn left up a short, narrow track.   Don't go all the way to the gate at the end but go over the stile in the RH hedge.   A used path goes straight up the hill, bearing very slightly left to pass the end of the LH hedge nearer the top.   Ignore it!   Before venturing up the hill, locate a single electricity pole slightly to your right over the brow of the hill.   Then check the position of the top end of the LH hedge where the unwanted path goes.   What you want is a direction where the pole is 1/5 off to your right and the top end of the hedge is 4/5 off to your left (or 82 degrees East if you still have your compass).

Off you go - and you should arrive, somewhat breathless, at a stile in the top hedge which runs parallel to the road.   There will be a farm gate in the field corner, about 20 yards to your right.

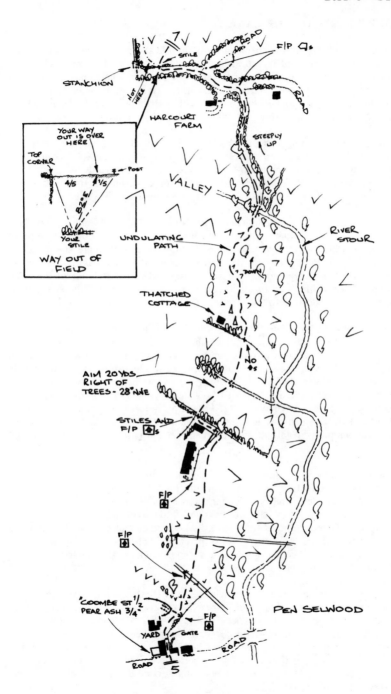

F/P ⌐s

STILE

STANCHION

NOT
HERE

ROAD
P.O.

ROAD

HARCOURT
FARM

STEEPLY
UP

TOP
CORNER

YOUR WAY
OUT IS OVER
HERE

POST

4/5   1/5

82°E

YOUR
STILE

WAY OUT OF
FIELD

VALLEY

RIVER
STOUR

UNDULATING
PATH

DOWN

THATCHED
COTTAGE

NO
4s

AIM 20YDS
RIGHT OF
TREES - 28°NNE

STILES AND
F/P ◈s

F/P ◈

F/P ◈

PEN SELWOOD

"COOMBE ST ½
PEAR ASH ¾"

YARD   GATE

F/P ◈

ROAD

ROAD

5

151

DAY 6 - STAGE 7

HARCOURT FARM TO TOP LANE

At the stile, you will see that the arrow on the stile and the pointer on the other side both indicate exactly the right direction back to the stile at the bottom of the field. Turn left along the tarmac lane with a wide verge and ditch on your right. Near a left turn, go up the Bridleway-signed tarmac track on the right - at an angle to the road. At its end, when the track turns off to the right with a Bridleway arrow, keep straight on through 1.1/2 gates (with Bridleway and Footpath arrows) into a very long field.

Keep to the cut grass, slightly rising, track alongside the LH hedge and, after 150 yards, you will have distant views of high downland across the field to your right. Enjoy the lovely views of the high downs from your grassy, 510 yards long levelling track. Then, with a left/right wiggle, your wide track becomes entrained between high mixed beech, elderberry and hawthorn hedges for another 570 yards.

Suddenly, the track opens out a little where a gate on the RH corner leads into the field behind the hedge. A Footpath arrow points back down your track as you step out carefully onto a tarmac road. Over the opposite, high stone wall there stands a fine' stone house. This is Bonham where you turn left down the road, passing a concrete turning with a Footpath arrow pointing into the farmyard on the RH side of the road. Keep straight on down the road for another few yards and then take the steep, right Footpath-signed track down into the woods.

Descending somewhat, the main track bears right after a Footpath-arrowed kissing gate leads into the RH field. A sign excludes horse riders without permits from using any more of the track and this, I would suppose, leaves the other riders with no option but to turn back - because the steeply descending path which turns off to the left is only a Footpath - not a Bridleway. However, when you begin your way down this steep, stony, nettle-blessed path, you will be struck by the erosion being caused by numerous iron-shod feet. Anyway, whilst watching where you put your own feet, you will notice that the steep path has new trees planted on its left side whilst it has foxgloves and campion brightening its route down the edge of a mixed pine and deciduous wood.

Arriving at the bottom, with a confirmation Footpath arrow, you emerge onto a road. Now, for those who would like to go straight into Stourton village for The National Trust's Stourhead Gardens, Tea Rooms and the Spread Eagle Inn, the road going to the right will lead you there. In the Gardens, you will find two of the springs which feed Stourhead lake. These are beautifully staged with statues and grottoes but they are not the primary source of the Stour. This privilege belongs to the higher lakes which you will find at Six Wells Bottom - and you will come back round to the village afterwards on Stage 9, anyway.

However, looking that way, past a pond which is fed by the infant River Stour, you will see an old farm cottage with a walled garden and a few barns. Cross over the road and walk down the lane opposite, signed 'Top Lane. Private Road'. At first, the fields on either side are well below the level of this banked road. After opposing farm gates, the River Stour flows under the road from the pond on the right and through the remains of a small brick and stone building on the left. From here, the gravel track ascends quite steeply with a deep wood beyond a fenced ditch on the left and the lower field still on your right.

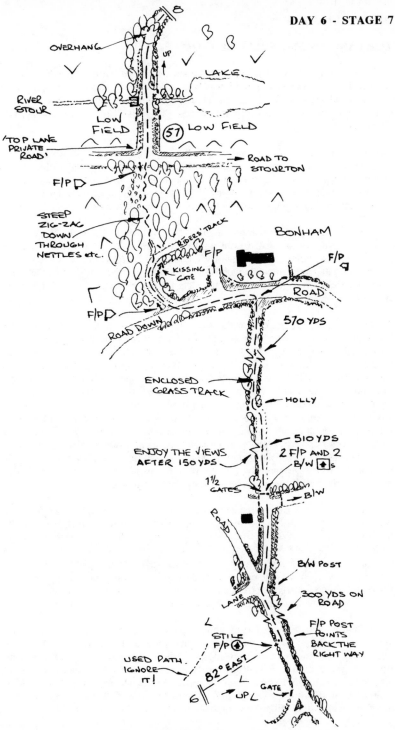

OVERHANG

UP

LAKE

RIVER STOUR

LOW FIELD

57 LOW FIELD

'TOP LANE PRIVATE ROAD'

ROAD TO STOURTON

F/P

STEEP ZIG-ZAG DOWN THROUGH NETTLES etc.

RIDERS' TRACK

F/P

BONHAM

F/P

KISSING GATE

ROAD

F/P

ROAD DOWN

570 YDS

ENCLOSED GRASS TRACK

HOLLY

ENJOY THE VIEWS AFTER 150 YDS

510 YDS

2 F/P AND 2 B/W ♠s

1½ GATES

B/W

ROAD

B/W POST

300 YDS ON ROAD

LANE

F/P POST POINTS BACK THE RIGHT WAY

STILE F/P ♠

USED PATH IGNORE IT!

82° EAST

6 ‖

UP

GATE

DAY 6 - STAGE 8

TOP LANE TO SIX WELLS BOTTOM

Still walking uphill, past the 'Private Woods. No Dogs' sign, past some lofty pines and beeches on your left and past a row of small ash trees and a hedge on your right, the lane suddenly turns left.   At this bend, go through the gate which keeps you on a straight line and into the open field beyond.   There isn't a Footpath arrow but there should be.

Down on your right, you now get your first glimpse of the edge of Stourhead Gardens whilst thick woods carpet the valley and hills opposite.   In the Domesday Book, Stourton had a forest "one league long and one league wide".   Ahead of you, up to your left is Top Wood.   Aim about 25 yards to the right of the far RH edge of the wood, keeping to the upper slopes of the park at first (due North).

Arriving at the top of the slope, begin to bear a little to the right as you begin to descend, aiming to pass just to the right of a single oak.   Now, aim for a wooden signpost which stands on the edge of the main gravel track, near a track which turns off up to a gate in the opposite woods.   Turn left on the main gravel track and head uphill for the sharp right turning to the slate-roofed, stone cottage with the sculptured front hedge - Beech Cottage.

A little further up the track, near the top, you will find a wicket gate in the fence and hedge after the track from the cottage.   Before you enter the steeply rising wood, you have another view of Alfred's Tower in the near distance.   This red-brick folly was built by Henry Hoare II, the instigator of the development of the garden with its idyllic landscape of classical temples, bridges, grottoes, sculptures, monuments and rare species of trees and plants.   Through the gate, begin a cautious ascent through the new trees - on the path if there is one now - aiming for the top right of the hill. After passing almost above Beech Cottage, the path continues until it crosses a grass forest track which comes in from the left and a notice proclaims 'No Riders' on your right.   Keep straight on upwards, through beeches and pines, crossing another track before emerging onto an amazingly wide and grassy ride which leads from the Gardens to Park Hill fort.   Apparently, it's this wide for game shooting.   It gives the guns plenty of time to kill the pheasants as they are driven across the gap.

Turn left along the ride and keep straight on, through copper beeches, beeches, chestnuts, oaks, ash, pine, sessile oaks, rhododendrons, ferns, bluebells and foxgloves etc., for about 250 yards.   Then turn right onto another grassy track which is only about 60 yards long.   At its end, turn left onto the last track. Carefully pace out 15 yards along this track and then step into the trees on your right. There may be a small seat marking the beginning of the steeply descending, root-filled path down through the trees and bracken.   This is the equivalent descent to the ascent from the wicket gate up into these woods, so it's not a short path.

At the bottom end, you come onto another path which runs to the right, above a small lake.   Turn onto it for a few yards and it then joins a bigger path which comes from the Gardens on your right.   There is an arrow on the reverse side of a post on your right.   Join the main path as it turns, between two of the source lakes, to a Footpath-arrowed stile in a wire fence.   Over the stile - *You are in Six Wells Bottom - The source of the River Stour!*   From here, the path runs very slightly right across the valley to a stile in the opposite fence - at 40 degrees NE.

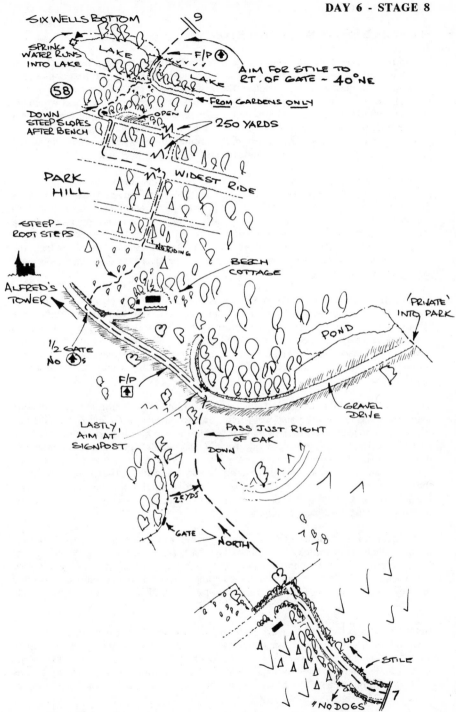

SIX WELLS BOTTOM

SPRING WATER RUNS INTO LAKE

LAKE

F/P

LAKE

9

AIM FOR STILE TO RT. OF GATE ~ 40°NE

(58)

FROM GARDENS ONLY

DOWN STEEP SLOPES AFTER BENCH

OPEN

250 YARDS

PARK HILL

WIDEST RIDE

STEEP ROOT STEPS

NO RIDING

BEECH COTTAGE

ALFRED'S TOWER

½ GATE NO ⊕s

F/P

POND

'PRIVATE' INTO PARK

GRAVEL DRIVE

LASTLY, AIM AT SIGNPOST

PASS JUST RIGHT OF OAK

DOWN

25 YDS

GATE

NORTH

UP

STILE

NO DOGS

7

155

DAY 6 - STAGE 9

SIX WELLS BOTTOM TO STOURTON

The hills on either side all drain into Six Wells Bottom although, beyond the first lake, the valley is dry. Rain percolates down through the chalky soil and comes into these lakes through springs. Before these were medieval fishponds, the springs would have been visible in the valley floor as are several remaining springs which are scattered among the wooded slopes and higher up the valley. Savour this moment and consider how all of the water which starts here will eventually pass through the lakes, under the bridges, through the mills, around the villages, into the towns and out into the English Channel in 58 miles from here (as you have walked).

So, exhilarated and regretful at the same time, head across the valley and up to the stile in the opposite fence, about 50 yards right of the wooden signpost for 'Alfred's Tower and Stourhead House'. Go over the Footpath-arrowed stile and turn right onto the track - but only for 10 yards. On your left, there is a wooden post sticking up out of the bracken with two Footpath arrows attached. Turn off the track and head up the faint path through the wooded slopes. As you reach the last few steps from the top of the slope, it becomes progressively steeper but then you arrive at a Footpath-arrowed stile in the fence .

Over the fence, there are smartly mowed lawns, a neat gravel driveway and a beautiful square, stone summer house all awaiting your arrival. You will see the Bath-stone Obelisk and Stourhead House away to your right. Walk up to the gravel and grass track and turn right, signed for 'Stourhead House'. The track becomes tarmac and grass as it traverses open parkland with some very old trees scattered about. At the far end of the long drive, go over a cattle grid onto a bending section of track with a wood on your right.

You soon reach another cattle grid which leads you into a small iron-fenced enclosure with open parkland facing you. Turn right, by a wooden signpost and go through the gate to join the main gravel driveway near the House with a wide lawn on its left hand side. Past the House, the drive swings round under a high bank of rhododendrons and past the Gardens entrance and yards on the right. As the drive swings back the other way, there are some ancient sessile oaks on the LH side where a Footpath comes back through the iron gate from the park. Down the drive, go through the stone arch with a gatehouse on the left and cross over the road, slightly to your left, to find the pedestrians' path for Stourton village.

Turn right onto the path and follow it down, parallel to the sunken road, to Stourton - for a celebratory cream tea at the old village hall, drinks at the Spreadeagle Inn or thanksgiving at St Peter's church. If there's time after all that, why not pay a visit to the beautiful Gardens. Or come back another day with some friends and astound them by quietly dropping into the conversation, "I've walked here from Christchurch, you know".

But what about St Peter's? Well, it dates from the 13thC and parts of the original nave and tower still remain. Much rebuilding was carried out in the 16thC and again after the Stourton estates were sold to the Hoare family in 1717. As usual, the Victorians carried out their own particular brand of restoration and, even as late as 1974, the old box pews were removed from the North aisle, the East end of which was made into a baptistry.

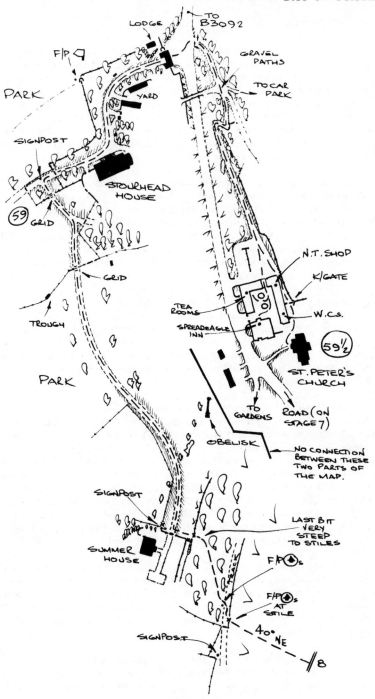

157

THE NEW STOUR VALLEY PATH

IN CONCLUSION

You will have realised by now that this isn't just a reprint of the old 'Stour Valley Path'. If you walked the original, you will have found that there are several totally new sections on this revised route and even the possibility of a lovely circular walk thrown in for good measure. Conscious that Day 4 in the 1st edition was probably too long for one day, I redesigned the whole layout so that the complete journey now takes six days instead of five and *every* day ends in, or within yards of, a town with major bus routes. Several readers have told me that they've walked the Stour Valley Path more than once already and it was a sheer delight for me to walk the whole route yet again (three more times, actually) - and to find some better paths on the way.

The New Stour Valley Path follows the River Stour from its headlong-rushing finale into the welcoming blue waters of the English Channel. It skirts around the edges of the holiday towns of Christchurch and Bournemouth. It ambles over rich arable and pasture land. It wanders through market towns and little villages. It passes mills and strolls along gentle vales. It climbs over, or meanders around, ancient hill forts and, eventually, it arrives at the source of the River Stour in the dry valley of Six Wells Bottom. What a wonderful walk it is. I have stored up even more memories from these latest explorations and can't wait for an excuse to go again.

Everybody who completes the Stour Valley Path takes home memories of one section which is more special to them than any other. It may have been a sudden unexpected view, a peaceful village church, a dappled pool of sunlight under a cluster of shady trees or a flashing kingfisher on the river. Or maybe, you will have met a 'local' and passed a few pleasant moments in conversation. There are so many delights along The Stour Valley Path that it seems to epitomise much of what this lovely country of ours has to offer.

As we have passed along the way, alone or in groups, great houses (and some that have seen better days), village churches and wayside inns have drawn us to them whilst cattle and sheep have watched us carefully as we have traversed their home pastures. We have heard village tales which have been handed down through generations of Dorset folk and we have learned some of the history of the villages and towns which cling to this beautiful river's edges. I still can't quite lay my finger on what it is about The Stour Valley Path that says, "This is the real England - how can anybody ever leave?". It's all very well to travel and see other exciting countries and to find out how other people live their lives but isn't it good to get back to England? Many an expatriate is haunted, like Robert Browning, by longings for home. You know, "Oh, to be in England, now that April's there" and all that.

From Blandford Forum Northwards, this has been a wander through William Barnes' country. It's hardly any different from Barnes' day and he would surely still feel at home here even if modern farming methods have brought about superficial changes to the landscape. The people are mostly the same and I'm sure that, as you've passed through some of the little villages on your way, you will have passed cottages where, just as in Barnes' day:

> *"the maidens do stan' out in clusters avore*
> *the doors, vor to chatty an' zee vo'k goo by"*
> ...from "Blackmore by the Stour"

158

ACKNOWLEDGMENTS

First and foremost, I would like to thank the delectable Janet, my wife and best friend, who has shared some of my excursions and provided me with succulent picnics for my lone days. A sandwich and a Granny Smith are a feast under Dorset skies.

Special thanks go to North Dorset District Council Stour Valley Ranger, Clare Freeman for her ever-cheerful help and to N.D.D.C. legal eagle Jacqui Andrews for patiently sorting out all of my Footpath queries.

I would like to thank everybody who has written to me after completing the first 'Stour Valley Path' to say that the book was like having a companion on the walk. That is exactly what I wanted. All of these books are written for just one person - the gentleman or lady who will be following behind me. I want him or her to see what I have seen and not to get lost. With the guide notes, I want everybody to be able to concentrate on enjoying all there is to see without worrying about losing the way.

BIBLIOGRAPHY

History and Antiquities of the County of Dorset: Rev John Hutchins 1861-64
Dorset Churches: Sir Owen Morshead: Dorset Historic Churches Trust 1976
William Barnes: Alan Chedzoy: Dovecote Press 1985
Inventory of Historic Monuments in the County of Dorset: HMSO 1970
Highways and Byways in Dorset: Sir Frederick Treves: Macmillan 1914
The Old Roads of Dorset: Ronald Good 1966
Dorset - Upalong and Downalong: Ed. Marianne R Dacombe: D F W I 1935

INDEX

East Farm, Hammoon: 102
East View Farm, Bourton: 146
Eccliffe: 134
Edmunds. Mr: 14
Edward of Salisbury: 44
Eloy, Saint: 86
Enclosure Acts: 88,146
Exton Road: 18
Eye Bridge: 50,52

Falaise, William de: 140,144
Feltham Farm, Silton: 144
Fiddleford: 102,104
Fiddleford Mill: 104,106
Fifehead Magdalen: 124,126
Fillymead. Marnhull: 124
Firs Farm, Cowgrove: 52
FitzGrip, Hugh: 40
Forum View, Bryanston: 80
Four Winds Farm, Throop: 26
Fox and Hounds, Canford: 42
Freke, William: 116
Fudge, Mrs (and the witch): 122

Gaunt, John of: 44
Georges III and IV: 26
Gillingham: 136
Glebe, The, Durweston: 86
Godmund. Thane: 140
Gotts Corner, Stur. Newton
Gravel Lane, Charlton Marshall: 72
Grove Field, Marnhull
Guest, Sir John: 44
Guides, Girl: 34

Hall and Woodhouse: 76,136
Ham Down Copse: 100
Ham Lane, Canford: 40,42
Hambledon Hill: 12,90,92,94,96
Hammoon: 102,104
Hammoon Manor: 102
Hampreston: 40
Hanford: 88
Hanging, The, Bryanston: 84
Harcourt Farm: 150,152
Hardwick P C. Architect: 86
Hardy, Thomas: 78
Harold, King: 140
Haycombe, Durweston: 86
Hayden Farm, Plummer: 108
Harpitts Bridge: 130
Hastings, Battle of: 102
Havelins, Stourpaine: 88

Hayden Bridge, Plummer
Haywards Bridge: 96,102
Haywards Lane, Child Okeford: 96
Hengistbury Head: 10,12
Henry VIII: 64,124
Heron Court: 22
High Street, Child Okeford: 96
High Street, Gillingham: 136
High Street, Shapwick: 56
Hinton St Mary: 112,114,116,118
Hoare Family, Stourhead: 156
Hod Drive, Stourpaine: 88,90
Hod Hill: 12,90,92
Holdenhurst: 18,22,24
Holdenhurst Farm: 22
Holdenhurst Road: 24
Home Farm, Bryanston: 82
Home Farm, Stourton: 156
Hopkins, Rev: 24
Hurn Airport: 20
Hurn Court School: 22,24
Hutchins. Rev J: 96,122,136,144
Hyde Farm, Shapwick: 56

Iford: 14,16
Iford Bridge: 16,18
Iford Lane: 16
Isle of Purbeck: 10
Isle of Wight: 10
Iwerne Minster: 92

Jacob's Ladder, Child Okeford: 96
John of Gaunt: 44
Julians Road, Wimborne: 50

Kahaines, Ralph de: 64
Kefton, Will: 24
Kentisworth Road, Marnhull: 122
Keynston Mill: 66,68
Kings College, Cambridge: 128
Kingston Lacy: 54,56
Knighton House & School: 86

Lady Wimborne's Drive: 44,46
Lake Gates: 48
Lake Farm: 50
Layard, Sir Austin: 44
Leicester, Earl of: 58
Lenin: 16
Little Canford: 42
Little Cowgrove Common: 54
Littleton: 72,74
Littleton Farm: 74

Spread Eagle Inn, Stourton: 157
Stapehill: 42
Station Road, Stur. Newton: 108,112
Stocking Bridge: 144,146
Stour Close, Little Canford: 40
Stour Inn, Blandford St Mary: 80
Stour Prospect Viewpoint: 46
Stour Provost: 124,126,128
Stour Provost Mill: 126
Stourbank Gardens, Little Canford: 40
Stourhead and House: 152,154,156
Stourpaine: 86,90
Stourton: 122,152,156
Stourton Lane: 156
Straight, Rev John: 88
Stroud Common: 146
Stur. Newton: 94,102,106,108,112,118
Swanage: 10
Sweetbriar Drove, Kingston Lacy: 54,56

Tarrant Crawford: 60,64,66
Tarrant Crawford Abbey: 64
Tchertkov, Count: 16
Thorkel: 40
Thorngrove: 134,136
Throop: 24
Throop Fisheries: 20,24
Throop Mill: 20,24,26,30
Todber: 124
Tolstoy, Leo: 16
Top Lane, Stourton: 152,154
Tuckton: 14,16
Tuckton Road: 16
Twinwood Coppice: 114,116

Uddens: 40
Upper Street, Child Okeford: 96
Upton Lane, Blandford St Mary: 74

Valley Road, Throop: 24
Vespasian: 12
Vintner's Fee: 58,60
Vynere, Walter de: 58,60
Wake, Archbishop: 58
Walnut Farm, Cowgrove: 52
Walnut Tree Farm, Eccliffe: 134
Walter of Eureux: 44
Watch House, Mudeford: 10
Waymarking: 3
West End, Spetisbury: 68
West Stour: 128,130
Whistley Farm and Water: 142
White Horse, Hinton St Mary: 116
Wick Fields and Village: 12,14
Willett Road, Merley: 48,50
Wimborne Minster: 52,56
Wimborne Road, Wimborne: 50
Wimborne, Lady: 44
Winterbourne Stickland: 80
Wood Lane, Hinton St Mary: 118
Wyatt, James. Architect: 80,82,84,88
Wyndham, Sir Hugh: 144
Wyke: 136
Wyke, Richard de: 136

Yardgrove Farm: 118,120
Yeomans Road, Throop: 24

Zeals: 142,146

PERSONAL LOG